Scrap City

Scrapbooking for Urban Divas

and Small-Town Rebels

Scrap City

Scrapbooking for Urban Divas and Small-Town Rebels

I would like to thank my beautiful wife, Martine. She deserves the best—but got me instead. And to my little boy, Anthony, whose wonderful smile is a daily source of inspiration. I love you both dearly.

sixth&spring books

Sixth&Spring Books
233 Spring Street
New York, New York 10013

Editorial Director
Trisha Malcolm

Art Director
Chi Ling Moy

Graphic Designer
Sheena Thomas

Technical Editor
Fiona Connolly

Copy Editors
Susan Edgar
Pamela Grossman

Book Division Manager
Erica Smith

Production Manager
David Joinnides

President and Publisher,
Sixth&Spring Books
Art Joinnides

Library of Congress Cataloging-in-Publication Data

Library of Congress Control Number: 2005934950
ISBN 10: 1-931543-93-3
ISBN 13: 978-1-931543-93-4

Manufactured in China

3 5 7 9 10 8 6 4

First Edition, 2006

Photography by Dan Howell

"Madness" by Bonnie Woolger

CONTENTS

"Does This Make My Thighs Look Fat?" by Leah Blanco Williams p.153

FOREWORD

Scrap City was written for the thousands of stylish-city-dwelling and hip country-living women who are turned off by scrapbooking's good girl reputation. We felt it was time to say goodbye to smiley faces and teddy bears. You'll find no sunflowers, puppy dogs, or corny sentiments lurking in the back alleys of *Scrap City*.

Our goal? To inspire you to slip on your cutest shoes and hit the hot asphalt of *Scrap City* running. And how do we intend to accomplish such a feat? Well, our first objective was to smash scrapbooking's well-earned reputation as an un-hip craft. So, from here on in, we will refer to scrapbooking as an art form—which, in many respects, it truly is.

Step two was to round up an eclectic "gang" of unconventional scrapbookers and let them run wild. Artists from every walk of life and from around the world loaned their creative talents, and with a few quick turns of a page you will get to see the results. The layouts range from slightly edgy to completely outside the page. In fact, some have no page at all; the layouts were created digitally.

In addition to sussing out their artwork, we give you a moment, albeit brief, to "meet" the artists. In many cases, you'll find out just what motivated them to create the pieces shown in this book. Hey, it's always great to put a face to a work of art. *Scrap City* is not a "How-To" book, but we do feel it's important to give you a basic primer in the art of scrapbooking—show you some of the ins and outs of navigating through the rough-and-tumble world of Big City Scrapbooking.

And what better way to learn than from the pros? Read'em and keep'em, as many of the contributing artists spill their guts and let you in on the hippest tips and techniques to get your layouts cool and couture. There's also a 30-Minute Scrapbook, for all the girls out there who may want to squeeze a scrapbook in during their lunch break. And hey, at 30 minutes, you'll still have time to grab a latté.

We hope you enjoy the book. It was our pleasure to bring it to you.

ACKNOWLEDGMENTS

This book never could have happened without the talented artists who contributed their layouts to *Scrap City*. Your time, effort, and cooperation were greatly appreciated. And thanks to everyone at SOHO Publishing—they had faith in the concept, always smiled in meetings, and never hassled me.

I sincerely thank you all.

"I Believe" by Elsie Flannigan

INTRODUCTION

"Wouldn't be caught dead." "Shoot me if I ever." "Who, me?"

If any of these phrases were ever connected to you and your thoughts on scrapbooking, then you've come to the right place. Put those images of unicorns, rattles, and poorly drawn baseballs out of your head. *Scrap City* is the punk rocker of the scrapbooking world; the black sheep of the craft society; the glue, scissors, and ruler from the wrong side of the tracks . . . all with a heart of gold. Or maybe not. It's up to you.

You are the new breed of scrapbookers—the ones who will learn all the rules, master them, and then systematically choose which ones to follow and which to break. You are the rebels with a glue stick in one hand and an unconventionally cropped photo of Uncle Harry in the other. Now that you've made the commitment, there is no turning back. Trust us. You will never regret this day.

Scrapbooking, no matter how nontraditional, can be very rewarding both artistically and emotionally. We've all had people and moments in our lives that warrant posterity, and now is your chance to ensure they do live on. Whether it's that rat-bastard boyfriend who broke your heart and stole your credit card, or that favorite scarf your Aunt Nettie knitted for you when you turned thirteen: If it demands a place in history, good or bad, happy or sad, you will soon have the inspiration to scrap it into eternity. Well, maybe not eternity, but for years to come, at least.

So, now that you know where you stand in the world of scrapbooking there's one more twist to the *Scrap City* theory of scrapbooking — You as the director.

Scrap City takes a filmmaker's approach to constructing a scrapbook. As the scrapbooker, you assume the role of director and/or screenwriter in unveiling your story—the key word there being story. Love it or hate it, one must admit that Hollywood has mastered the art of the "visual story," and these same techniques work just as well with scrapbooking. Here's your chance for that inner Quentin Tarantino to rear its creative head.

Some of the concepts we will discuss are: the importance of developing a theme or focus early on; steps to give your scrapbook a beginning, middle, and end; learning how to pick only the best images to use; determining the length of your scrapbook; and the benefit of thumbnail sketches in designing your pages. These techniques will help raise your scrapbook from a mere collection of snapshots and memorabilia to a true artistic statement.

There you have it. I hope you're ready, 'cause you're about to break new ground. Sure, you're going to make enemies. Other scrapbookers will scoff at you and whisper behind your back; some may even take your rubber stamps out of alphabetical order. The craft world can be a cruel place, but we're sure with these new-found skills, you can handle it.

Have fun. Break the rules. Over and out.

MEET THE ARTISTS

SCRAP CITY

Author seeks artists to create hip, unconventional scrapbooks to be featured in a book being released by a major publishing house.

Please contact me at urbanscrap.aol.com and I will email you more details.

From the initial conception of this book, I felt that the artist who created his or her work was as important as the work itself. I wanted to give the reader the opportunity to put a face to the layout that he or she loved, hated, or was intrigued by—a chance to learn a little something about the artist, to find out what motivated each artist to create such a piece, and even get some tips and techniques for scrapbooking.

So when the call went out for unconventional scrapbooks and responses came from such a vast array of people, I couldn't have been more pleased. Everyone from unemployed artists to stay-at-home moms to fire-eating freak-show performers answered the call. This was exactly what I was hoping for.

Granted, this eclectic group of contributors made for a unique series of organizational "situations," and some of these may be reflected in the following pages. However, this only added to and emphasized the contributors' wonderful individuality.

the bump: up close and

personal

4 months

③

here comes 3

baby no. 3

THE BUMP

MOTIVATION

"The Bump" was one in a series of layouts documenting my friend's 3rd pregnancy. She is American but has a very favorite home-decorating magazine that's published in the UK, and they refer to a pregnant belly as a "bump." I thought it funny to refer to her belly as the bump, which also serves as a reference to her love of the British terminology in that magazine.

TIPS AND TECH

Create monochromatic look by layering digital cardstock of similar color. "Tear" large mat and create stitches.

Layer patterned paper, black mat, and photos. Attach date tab and photo corners and add subtext (baby no. 3, etc.). Add title and the look of hand-painting to distress layout.

SUPPLIES

Papers from monochromatic collection at www.gauchogirl.com. Fonts: My own handwriting (using Wacom pen tablet), Times New Roman, LD notepad (letteringdelights.com), MA Sexy (altered to look distressed) by Margarete Antonio.

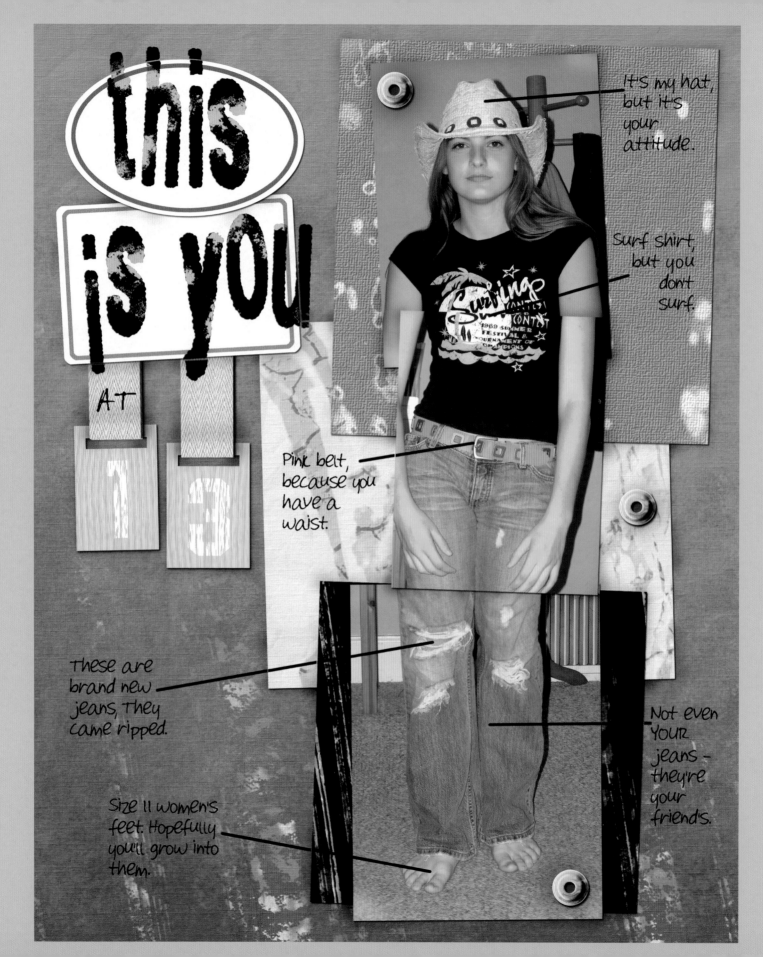

this

is you

AT

1 3

It's my hat, but it's your attitude.

Surf shirt, but you don't surf.

Pink belt, because you have a waist.

These are brand new jeans, They came ripped.

Not even YOUR jeans - they're your friend's.

Size 11 women's feet. Hopefully you'll grow into them.

THIS IS YOU AT 13

MOTIVATION

I wanted to document my daughter's "look" as she was transitioning out of child-hood. I chose to use 3 separate photos layered to form the one photo unit, to help show the disjointed feeling that one often goes through in puberty—the inability to fit in the category of child or of adult.

TIPS AND TECH

Digitally layer 3 squares of grungy-looking paper down right-hand side of back-ground. Crop photos to reveal basic body parts, and layer together to form one complete photo unit of body. Create title block with digital labels, foam stamp-look letters, twill, and wooden numbers. Use callout lines to highlight areas of photo unit with text.

SUPPLIES

All digital elements are from the planetEARTH collection on the URBANetc. CD from www.gauchogirl.com; Adobe Photoshop CS; Font: gauchogirl print.

Though not of South American descent, Tonya Doughty named her freelance digital-art studio "GauchoGirl Creative" (www.gauchogirl.com) to remind herself of the free spirit, independence, and hard-working nature of the South American cowboys known as Gauchos. A professional graphic designer, Doughty designs business cards, annual reports, and everything in between. She created her first digital scrapbooking layout in Fall 2003, and her work has since been published in specialty books and nearly every major scrapbook magazine in the United States. She also makes custom handmade albums, journals, and books, which are sold in gift stores and boutiques in the state of Washington.

'Right hand
Ribcage.

Please cross in
to the
cover existing ted.

Last we

designs

Left upper Arm.
Skin 'n Ink - Swansea - 1997.

Think it was taken from the
German Tribal Tattoo fair '95.

Going to be tatted over with
large Celtic Cross.

TATTOOS

MOTIVATION

I really wanted to compile a book of Royston's tattoos for him, so he'd have a book to document where he had them done, any reasons for them, any stories, etc. He also has a lot of designs that he would like tattooed in the future and wanted somewhere to store them all. I have constructed the book in such a way that more pages can be added as he gets more tattoos.

TIPS AND TECH

The mini book is made from greyboard covered with Basic Grey and Bazzil cardstock. For the title on the front cover, I used Bazzil cardstock cut into squares, stamped the letters, and then used 2 coats of diamond glaze to coat them. Once this was completely dry, I bent the squares to crack the diamond glaze.

For the designs page, I made a simple pocket from Basic Grey paper by using adhesive down the edges and along the bottom. I then used shipping tags for each design that Royston would like to have tattooed in the future and used a safety pin to secure them together.

The 'D' of design is an MM jigsaw letter covered in Basic Grey and coated with diamond glaze. I then used letter stickers for the rest of the word.

The remaining pages are Basic Grey and Bazzil cardstock, with the notes of each tattoo handwritten onto shipping tags.

SUPPLIES

Cardstock: Bazzil Basics. Patterned Papers: Vagabond by Basic Grey. Letter stamps: Art Warehouse by Creative Imaginations. Making Memories Jigsaw alphabet: poolside. Letter stickers: Pebbles Inc. Pen: Zig. Other: Shipping tags, safety pin, book rings.

Michelle Solomon

Michelle Solomon is twenty-five years old and lives in the United Kingdom with her boyfriend, Royston, two cats, and a puppy. She started scrapbooking two years ago and hasn't looked back since. Solomon loves experimenting with new products and innovative elements, and considers her style to be eclectic. "I really enjoy scrapbooking my travels to Australia and Bali, my pets and days out," she says. "I feel that it's important to include details about myself and my everyday life in my albums. I would have loved to know what my great-grandmother's favorite things were!" Solomon regularly teaches scrapbooking classes and also does freelance writing for a U.K. scrapbooking company.

SEASIDE FROLIC

MOTIVATION

Loose Ends is known for its edgy, fantasy-like style. It was pure frolic when this Loose Ends scrapbook page was designed. All of the fibers are natural with the antique postcard (circa 1912-1915) colored in by hand.

TIPS AND TECH

Cut handmade paper to 12" X 12". Hot glue paper braid around exterior edges; hold in place until firm. Use water-soluble glue and place picture in center of paper. Place abaca "Seafoam" ribbon over bottom of picture and use small glue dots to secure. Take abaca twine ("Hunter") to frame around picture; adhere. Repeat abaca twine "Natural" next to "Hunter" twine; secure. Repeat again with "Cinnamon" color abaca twine. Glue five tiny shell potpourri in left corner.

SUPPLIES

Loose Ends 26682 Handmade Island Fiber Paper "Sealife" (Loose Ends 24" X 36"—makes 6 12" x 12" sheets). Loose Ends 09101—Paper Braid. Loose Ends 36009—Abaca Twine "Natural." Loose Ends, 36038—Abaca Twine "Cinnamon." Loose Ends 36033—Abaca Twine "Hunter."

Sandi Reinke—artist, designer, author, and owner of Loose Ends (an innovative company that designs, sources and manufactures handmade paper and other natural materials)—has been involved in creative endeavors since she was three years old. Raised in Southern California by a creative mother and a father who was a collector, Reinke developed a style that has become distinctly Loose Ends: unique, natural, and edgy. She lives with her husband, Art, in Salem, Oregon. Visit Sandi's Web site at www.looseends.com.

He was born on the streets of Brooklyn...

In order to simulate the experience of living with Brody...

step on these with your bare feet

(place on hardwood floor near litterbox, but somewhere they'll suprise you.)

now's he's...

my little roommate

Brody

He's the most mellow
and affectionate
cat I've ever known.
And also the
fattest!!

Writing songs...rehearsing...booking gigs...making flyers...distributing flyers...working on the Web site... it's a lot of work and we don't always agree...

but mostly we get along great and have a lot of fun together!

me
Lauren
Michele

An early version of our logo, drawn by my best friend and favorite tattoo artist JoAnn Atwood.

Bettie after midnight

in circulation since february 2005

TRUE GIRL STORIES
band bio & press clippings!

PEEPLAND
pics of the girls!

HOT LITTLE NUMBERS
listen to tracks!

LIVE GIRLS!
upcoming shows!

LOVE LETTERS
sign guestbook & send us e-mail!

SPEND A LITTLE DOUGH!
purchase cds and merch!

FOR A GOOD TIME
check out these hot links!

LET'S GO HOME TOGETHER
go back to the homepage!

Weclome to the all new *Bettie After Midnight* website!

We just completed our first ever album, *Exploits Of A Girl Gang*. Listen to some tracks in our music section!

Check out hot new pictures of the band taken by photographer Amy Chace!

Sign up for our mailing list so that you can stay on top of all *Bettie After Midnight* updates!

BRODY

MOTIVATION

Brody may be "just a cat," but he's got so much personality and he's so much fun to be with that he brings to life what would otherwise be a lonely little studio apartment in Brooklyn. I hope that comes across in these pages.

TIPS AND TECH

Besides photos, I wanted to include actual objects in these pages that would bring the subject to life. In the "Brody" pages, I used pieces of his cat food (which he loves even though it's the "diet" kind) and pellets from the fancy cat litter I get for him. These were glued on to the page and brushed with clear nail polish to help prevent flaking or crumbling. The photos were all taken with my camera phone during lazy weekend afternoons with Brody, which makes for grainy but candid images.

BETTIE AFTER MIDNIGHT

MOTIVATION

My band is a huge part of my everyday life, and it's something I'm excited about and want to share. People might view my band one way through our Web site, live shows, flyers, and other things that we put out there, but these scrapbook pages are about my personal experience of being in the band.

TIPS AND TECH

Instead of using only photos in the "Bettie After Midnight" pages, I included a flyer from one of our shows and a printout from our Web site. To give it a real-life feel, I included a worn-out guitar pick that I used at shows and practices and fishnet stockings as borders for some of the photos. I wrote all the text with a silver marker on scraps of black vinyl. There was a lot of careful cutting involved in this layout; getting that perfectly even white border around the logo and lining up cut after cut with craft scissors on sticky black masking tape are no easy feats.

I grew up one train stop outside Manhattan, where I could see the skyline from any corner. I wasn't sheltered from the ugly things in life, but I was able to learn lessons from bad events and make use of little advantages, like getting to study piano for twelve years. In the last five years, I've done a lot of things I always wanted to do: get a master's degree in film production and media studies at New York University, move to Hollywood to try my luck at becoming a movie star, run my own stand-up comedy show, learn to play new instruments, and get a job that keeps me from worrying about rent and food. Now I make my living as a writer and graphic designer—and spend the rest of my time as an aspiring rock star.

ITALY 2001

MOTIVATION

My girlfriend Sue and I had made plans to meet my son Don in Italy in October 2001, three weeks after the World Trade Center was attacked.

The political atmosphere was, as expected, very strange. I would peek at newspaper headlines to see what was going on in the world, occasionally buying one to catch a few details. The US government started bombing Afghanistan. While walking from the train station in Florence, we crossed paths with angry marchers calling for peace. It was my first trip to Europe and a very strange time to be a tourist. We certainly enjoyed our steady diet of pizza and gelato, and cruising the canals of Venice. But the knowledge that thousands of people's lives had just been lost, and that another war was being waged, was woven into each adventure.

TIPS AND TECH

I used an old cardboard children's book for the base of this project. The original pages should be sanded or the top layer of shiny paper peeled off. This helps the layers stick to the book. I saved newspapers and a magazine from our trip and used these pages as a background for the entire piece. They were applied with a foam brush and gel medium.

I combined photos, newspaper clippings, copies of tickets, and illustrations I did while traveling. Those were also applied with gel medium. After all of the pieces were in place, I chalked to add color to the pages.

Note: If pages stick together, talcum powder works wonders!

SUPPLIES

Children's cardboard book, gel medium, foam brush, magazine, newspaper, copies of photos, tickets, chalk.
Photos by Donald Stillwell Booth

PARIS

MOTIVATION

My partner Midge and I took our daughter Sara Beth on a trip to Paris for her birthday. We traveled before her actual birthday, so I created a map page to give to her on her birthday as a memento of our special trip.

TIPS AND TECH

I started by piling up pictures and ephemera saved from the trip. I put it all out on the table and kept moving things around until they started to make some sense as a composition. After I came up with the idea of using the map as the surface for my page, it was just a matter of composing around that. I like to work very freely, adding and subtracting as I go. By using press type on the cover I could give it a personal touch, but it still gives the illusion that it was part of the original map. The computer is an important tool to resize pictures and to scan and print ephemera that you don't want to cut up.

SUPPLIES

Map, pictures, trip ephemera to include a folding map, press type, glue stick.

Artgirlz

Allison and Tracy Stillwell are creative and clever sisters who love working with cloth, paper, and threads. Most recently, they have put their creative energy into developing collage kits and pewter charms for their new enterprise, Artgirlz. They often incorporate political and personal messages into unpredictable combinations of cloth, paint, wood, beads, bones, clay, rope, twigs, yarns, and found objects. Their work has been featured in magazines and books, sold in museum shops and galleries, and exhibited nationwide. Practicing truth and gratitude—and snacking for strength—the Stillwell sisters continue down the path of their somewhat remarkable and very full lines.

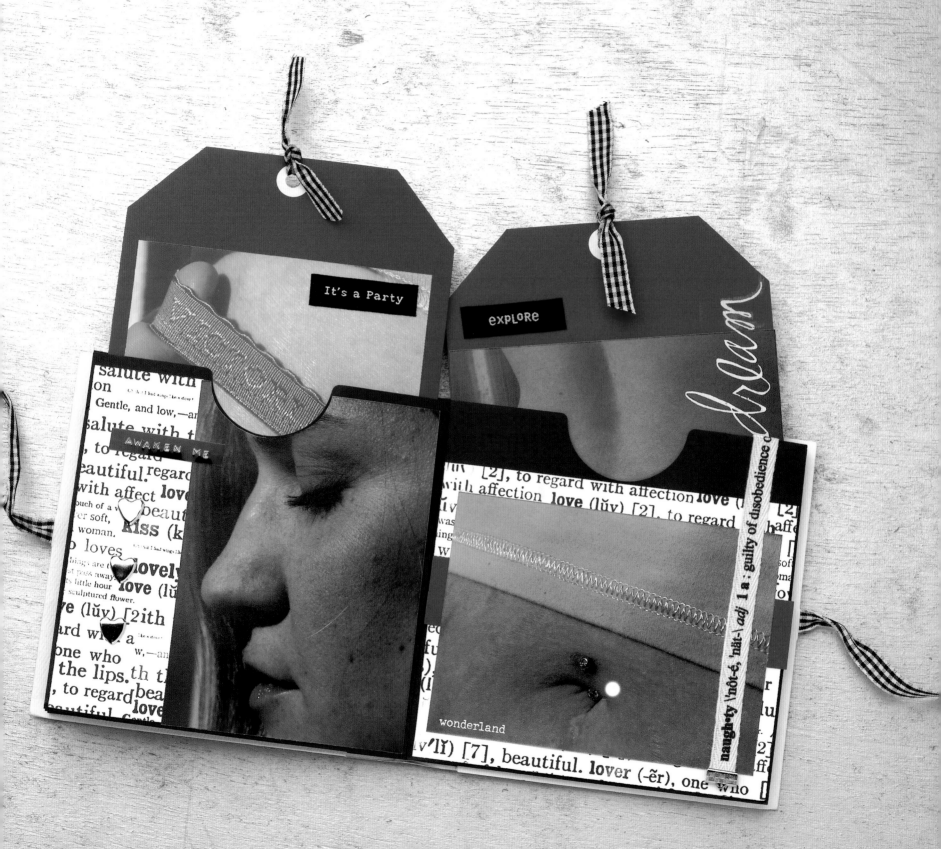

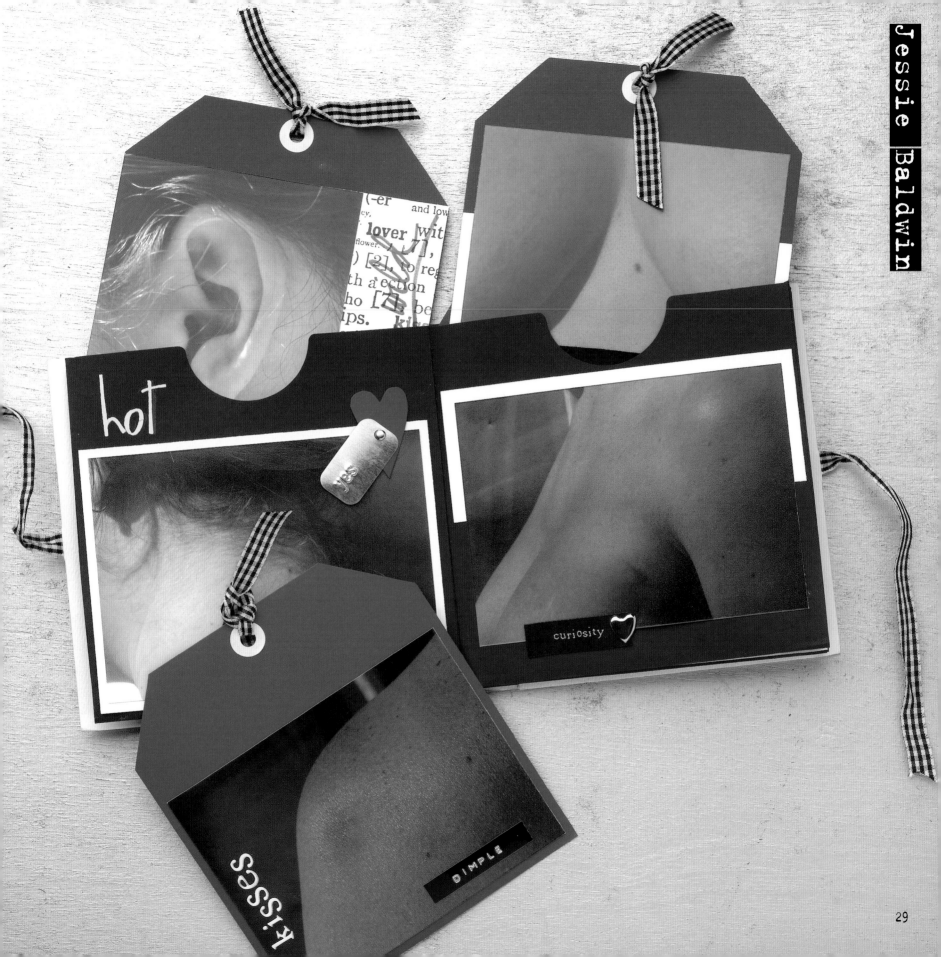

ALL THE WAY

SUPPLIES

Album: Making Memories Mini Pocket Album, 6" x 6"; Patterned Papers: 7Gypsies, Carolee's Creations; Metals and Rub-Ons: Making Memories; Woven Tags: Me & My BIG Ideas; Letter Stickers: Sonnets, Creative Imaginations; Word charm "kisses": Lil Davis; Hole Reinforcements: Avery; Ribbons: Offray; DYMO label maker, Poetry Dog Tags.

MOTIVATION

It was a Valentine's Day gift for my husband. I wanted to make him a scrapbook that wasn't all cutesy and sappy. I wanted it to be a little edgy and a little racy, and something he would want to reach for over and over again—something that would remind him of all the little parts of me that he loves.

TIPS AND TECH

I invited a close friend over to take the photos of me using my digital camera. We concentrated on different body parts that aren't usually associated with "racy" pictures but would excite my husband anyway — my shoulder dimple, the back of my neck, my knees, my panty line, my belly button, my lips... etc.—and printed them in black and white to give it a more moody, artsy feel (and hide my many flaws).
I started with a Making Memories 6" x 6" mini album—white cover with black pockets. Then I created the tags that would fit in the pockets out of red cardstock. All my accessories for this were black/white/red. I tried to choose words and phrases that might sound innocent in other settings but that totally changed connotation when put into the setting of this album. Assembly was quick and easy, as the main focus of each page was the photo itself.

Jessie Baldwin has always kept scrapbooks, but it wasn't until after her daughter was born in 2000 that her sometimes-hobby turned into an obsession. Trying to keep up with the sheer volume of photos she accumulated proved overwhelming, but Baldwin didn't want to stop her creative outlet. So she changed her philosophy. "I'll never be 'caught up,'" she says. "I'd rather just sit back and enjoy the process of turning my favorite photos and memories into art. The rest will be fine in albums." Baldwin has been recognized in several major industry contests and published in magazines such as *Creating Keepsakes, Scrapbooks, Etc., Memory Makers, Legacy Art Magazine, PaperKuts,* and *Scrapbook Trends.* She lives in Las Vegas with her husband, Rick, and two children, Violet and Riley.

Come Up and See Me Sometime

I Have a Secret

Guess Who's Pregnant?

Guess Who's the Daddy?

I Should Have Danced All Night

THE DATE

MOTIVATION

The inspiration for the layout "The Date" was girlfriends. I started my pages with two stamps, "Whispering" and "Guess Who's Pregnant?" The rest of the story then fell into place.

TIPS AND TECH

Gather your photos. Lay them out so they tell the story. You can always enlarge, reduce, or crop your pictures to fit the space you have available. Start with your color theme. I used Black, White, Taupe, Grey and, Pink. Gather a selection of papers that follow your theme, including different weights, finishes, and textures. I used the stripes to add color and texture to the pages. Using the stripes vertically complements the city theme and extends the story line off the page.

Start with two 12" x 12" pieces of taupe cardstock. Use two striped papers of different scales, so one section will pop and the other recede.

Crop your photos. Leave $\frac{1}{4}$" of white on all edges to frame them. Mount these on text weight black Stardreams; trim to $\frac{1}{4}$" all around.

Using your favorite Putting on the Ritz designs, stamp with Colorbox pigment ink on Stardreams paper. Emboss each image with superfine clear powder. Trim each stamped design to within $\frac{1}{4}$" of the image.

Frame each photo on a piece of black Stardreams text weight paper. Crop to a $\frac{1}{4}$" border all around. The photos are the star of the show, so lay them on the page first. Then select your stamped images and frame the photos. Overlap the images, keeping your corners square. Shift everything until you have a pleasing composition. Look at the whole page as an image, making sure the color, weight, and light are balanced.

Nearly done. Now place your images down on the page. I use a roll-on tape adhesive that is repositionable. Ask for a recommendation from your local scrapbook rubber stamp store. You can add embellishments at this time, keeping in mind the context of your page. You've just completed a beautiful story.

Jeri L. Fricke

Jeri L. Fricke was born in and spent her early childhood in Seattle, Washington, before moving to Issaquah, then a small town. After college, she returned to Issaquah to raise her family. She started Putting on the Ritz, an art-stamp company, with some input from her artist sons, Dave and PJ.

When Jeri lost her eldest son, her father told her that it would be years before she had a day of complete joy but that she could find some joy in every day. Her father gave sage advice. As she began her business and made other life-changing decisions, she would often think, "What would Dad recommend?" She continues to look for the joy, find it, and to share it.

LOOK into the Mermaids Mirror...

Bambi's EXOTIC TROPICAL BIRD Roxie
@ Sideshows By the Seashore
July 3rd - 10 fond

My Burlesque Show *

Coney Island Mermaid Parade
The year I Won! *

CONEY ISLAND

Mermaids come on land to find TRUE LOVE...

CONEY ISLAND MERMAID

MOTIVATION

I like to create atmospheres for my memorabilia. I save press clippings, photos, and invites to my shows, and then I make ocean- or aquarium-inspired scenes to showcase them.

TIPS AND TECH

I'm very flexible with my style for scrapping. I like using old-school techniques learned in grade school—like Elmer's glue and stickers! Perfection does not exist in my world. Anything goes. I like to make mermaid "paper dolls" out of photos of my friends.

I used the hole puncher on the unused photos and used the dots to construct an abstract tail.

SUPPLIES

On this page I used blue Saran Wrap to make a clear ocean wave, glitter, and sand from Coney Island's beach.

Bambi the Mermaid, Queen of Coney Island, is a performance and visual artist as well as a burlesque star. The highlight of her year is Coney Island's annual mermaid parade. ("Being a professional mermaid rocks!" she says.) New York City's answer to Mardi Gras, the parade features sexy topless mermaids and other glorious spectacles, such as dogs wearing lobster costumes. The rest of the year, Bambi spends her time modeling and producing her weekly sideshow at Coney Island's Burlesque at the Beach. She is also working on her own photo project, titled "Bambi: Freak Pin-ups"—a series of postmodern pin-up girls who are "beauty challenged" by conventional standards. Bambi's main focus in life is to have fun—and lots of it.

Every girl is beautiful.

Every girl is unique.

Every girl is sexy.

Every girl is complex.

Emma

Every Girl is a pinup.

CORINA

Live footloose and fancy free—
You won't be young forever.
Youth lasts about as long as
smoke.   Ecclesiastes 11:10 THE MESSAGE

word to Norma
comes as close to
performer and a
Throughout
and recordings
preparation and
Norma, like
And yet no one
intended us to.
I have great
which animate
her family, an
orchestra feel
me great res
percent of ou
beautiful, w
We all hav
ly. It
her.

imony
RLEANS,
dred and 60

They are a part of me, and I am a part of them... the way I collect piles of magazines, and line up my perfume bottles. I certain way... Sometimes when I drink coffee or get into a "current obsession" I just sit there and let it sink in just how deep they have made me who I am. Today I was looking at these old photographs of my grandmothers and I wish I could stay through time and watch their beautiful lives, their favorite songs, their passions, and the little things like their adventures, their soon I am going to be the girl in the photo-which isn't a fear pretty soon I am going to be the girl in the photo-which isn't a fear for me as much as it is a challenge to find out who I am and live out my own missia and to enjoy today. elicia

SPACE AGE MEETS COUNTRY CHIC

SUPPLIES

Paper: Daisy D's and EK Success. Metal Mesh: Making Memories. Letter Stamps: EK Success. Stamps: OCD, A Stamp in the Hand of Time, Vintage Lady, Dawn Houser. Ink: ColorBox. Pen: Sakura. Other: studs.

EVERY GIRL IS A PINUP

TIPS AND TECH

Here I took a large silk flower apart and used the individual blooms.

SUPPLIES

Cardstock: Bazzill. Ribbon: Offray. Foam Stamps: Making Memories. Other: flower, button, staples.

A PART OF ME

TIPS AND TECH

When working with non-acid-free products, I never use original photos. Use a reprinted version and make sure originals are kept in an acid-free environment.

Elsie Flannigan [MY BIO]

I started scrapbooking in the spring of 2004. I love to play with colors, textures and photography. I am also really involved in my art group (www. redvelvetart.com). I spend most of my free time creating and hanging out with my husband, T.J., and playing w/ my puppy, Cocoa.

INK ME

MOTIVATION

This page is about a tattoo I had done recently. It's a very simple layout, but I like how the photos pop out from the page.

TIPS AND TECH

I wanted to document this day by making a scrapbook page, and I decided to pay homage to the history of tattoos and the most famous tattooed culture — the Chinese. I purchased a Chinese newspaper at the local market and tore out bits of it to be incorporated with my color scheme of black, silver, and white. I taped all of my images to a 12" x 12" piece of chalkboard-colored paper, using double-stick archival tape.

Then I took soft handmade black paper that I had sprayed silver coloring on and made it into a sort of mix-and-match of black, white and silver all over the page with the Chinese newspaper.

To add accent to the pictures, I drew designs around them with a metallic silver marker. I purchased self-stick foam in black and white, and cut shapes from it to stick around the images. This gave a raised pearlescent quality to the accents, in the shapes of cherry blossoms (a very popular tattoo image).

In Photoshop I created the typed words "Tattoo" and "Ink Me" and printed them out with close-up photos of the tattoos. This page is very easy to make and shows how sometimes a simple color scheme can be eye-catching and bring more attention to your photographs.

SUPPLIES

Chinese newspaper, metal-foil paper, images from Photoshop on photopaper, silver marker.

As a multi-media performance artist, Amelia Winger-Bearskin draws on her Native American and Jewish backgrounds to blend new digital media and performance art with the traditional unifying qualities of storytelling. "With my scrapbook pages, I attempt to create a window into my life," she says. "I build environments that allow others to see not only what the people in the photos physically look like, but also the emotions, inspiration, and heritage they've brought to my life." Winger-Bearskin's one-of-a-kind performances and works of art have been featured in magazines, galleries, and theaters around the world. She is currently working toward her MFA in Transmedia/Experimental Film at the University of Texas at Austin. For more, visit www.StudioAmelia.com.

People
of the
Longhouse

PEOPLE OF THE LONGHOUSE

MOTIVATION

This page is in honor of my mother's family; I wanted to do a page about my family, but in a fresh way—a page to convey a sentiment that was both traditional and contemporary.

TIPS AND TECH

For my family, "traditional" means something similar to what our Seneca-Cayuga ancestors may have used in their arts and crafts. I decided I wanted to use as many natural elements as I could, combined with some that were simulated. Many beautiful, natural materials do not age well and can damage photographs, so be sure if you use these in your scrapbooking, that they do not contain natural acids or moisture.

I used cornhusk that was shredded and scraps of leather. I drew on the leather with permanent marker to make it appear to have been burned with markings. I painted a textured background piece of 12" x 12" paper with two colors of inexpensive acrylic craft paint to make it look like snake skin. Then I began to make layers for the pictures to "live" in, filled with cut pieces of paper, leather, straw that was braided, and beads that were glued down to make the "skin" appear to have been beaded.

I took some favorite family photos and using Photoshop, gave each of them harmonious color schemes to set the color tone for the entire page. I used pheasant feathers around the picture of my mother and her older sister and my son. Feathers in a native headdress could tell you what tribe that young man was from so, I felt it was nice to have them next to my son.

I had some of the photos raised up higher on beds of leather and some lower with cut paper and leather on top. This gave the images more depth and shape.

I used paint and shredded paper to frame and tie in each picture to the next. I used bits of plastic fake grass on the outside corner to give length to the outside edge of the paper, and I cut up the photograph of myself to make it connect better with the other images.

SUPPLIES

Leather cord and scraps found in scrap section of craft store. Corn husks. Beads, fake grass, pheasant feathers, Sharpie marker, acrylic craft paint.

Me and Jami

on the train

My best friend

Time for some flapper fun!

MY BEST FRIEND

MOTIVATION

In 2004 I moved to Dallas, and I didn't know a soul. It was strange getting used to Texas, having lived on the East Coast most of my life (now I have learned to love it here). One of the first few people I was fortunate to become friendly with was Jami Deadly, a model, Marilyn Monroe impersonator, and performer here in Dallas. One day we decided to get dressed up in the most fantastic flapper clothes we could manage and head down to the old steam-engine yard in downtown Dallas. The steam-engine museum has the most wonderful old locomotives and fully restored passenger cars. We took some fun photos at the museum and I wanted to remember this day with a scrapbook page.

TIPS AND TECH

Jami loves peacock feathers and says that they remind her of everything from the 1920s, so I was sure to make the entire page look like a peacock feather and also like an old glorious stage you might have performed on during that era.

I used a lot of items from costumes Jami and I had made in the past year for various performances we did together, including the peacock feather.

I started off with a piece of 12" x 12" paper and attached the photos to the page with double-stick archival tape and, I drew with gold marker to connect the two photos into one. Then I began to build up the page using fabric, paper, and finally some metal findings. I used fringe and pre-made beaded trim for the top with some stiff metallic paper.

I made the side curtains with ruffled lace, and the bottom with upholstery fabric and a bit of silver material I sewed onto a metal finding to resemble a ladies garter belt from the ('20s). I attached a gilded leaf, Peacock feather and plenty of rhinestones and sequins to bring to life this elegant tribute to my friendship with a fellow performer, Jami.

SUPPLIES

Gold necklace from thrift store. Bead trim, plastic rhinestones, old marker, peacock feather, metal findings.

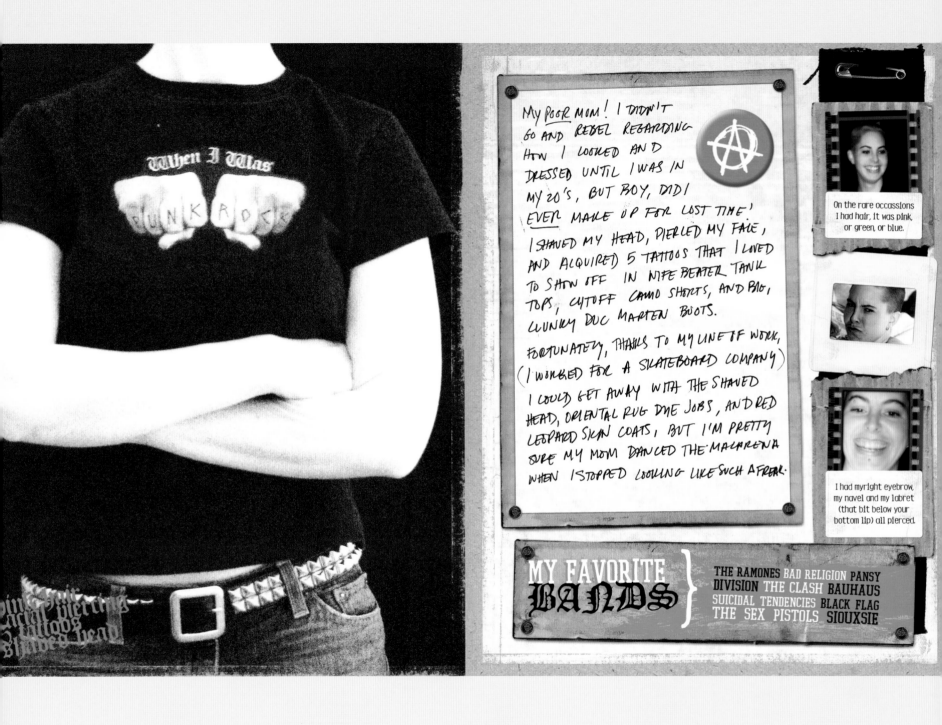

My POOR MOM! I DIDN'T GO AND REBEL REGARDING HOW I LOOKED AND DRESSED UNTIL I WAS IN MY 20'S, BUT BOY, DID I EVER MAKE UP FOR LOST TIME! I SHAVED MY HEAD, PIERCED MY FACE, AND ACQUIRED 5 TATTOOS THAT I LOVED TO SHOW OFF IN WIFE BEATER TANK TOPS, CUT OFF CAMO SHORTS, AND BIG, CLUNKY DOC MARTEN BOOTS.

FORTUNATELY, THANKS TO MY LINE OF WORK, (I WORKED FOR A SKATEBOARD COMPANY) I COULD GET AWAY WITH THE SHAVED HEAD, ORIENTAL RUG DYE JOBS, AND RED LEOPARD SKIN COATS, BUT I'M PRETTY SURE MY MOM DANCED THE MACARENA WHEN I STOPPED LOOKING LIKE SUCH A FREAK.

On the rare occassions I had hair, it was pink, or green, or blue.

I had my right eyebrow, my navel and my labret (that bit below your bottom lip) all pierced.

MY FAVORITE BANDS } THE RAMONES BAD RELIGION PANSY DIVISION THE CLASH BAUHAUS SUICIDAL TENDENCIES BLACK FLAG THE SEX PISTOLS SIOUXSIE

PUNK ROCK

MOTIVATION

I wanted to create a layout that reflected who I used to be — so many layouts I see in magazines are so "perfect," those '50s-sitcom images of blonde children and traditional families. My life just isn't like that. I've had a shaved head, a pierced face, and several tattoos. When I see a kid with a Mohawk I smile instead of scowl, and I'd still rather listen to the Transplants, the Vandals, and the Ramones than anything playing on a Top 40 station. I just wanted to pass on a story of what it was like to buck the norm and be my true self, proudly and with no regrets.

Chris Ford is not your average scrapbooker. A traditionally trained graphic designer disillusioned with Web design after the dot.com crash, she was considering a career change when she wandered fortuitously into a local scrapbooking store. It was love at first sight. Although Ford has always been a "crafty" person, it wasn't until she discovered scrapbooking's fusion of photography, design, and writing that she found her niche. Her pages reflect her unique outlook on life and tend to tackle such offbeat topics as political issues she feels strongly about, her reaction to major social change in her lifetime, and her tattoos.

ANTONIO

ANTONIO LOVE

```
SUPPLIES

Patterned Paper:
Zsiage—Asian Combo
and Setting Sun.
Vellum: Zsiage—Asian
Proverb. Cardstock:
Unknown,. Photo
Turns: 7 Gypsies.
Ribbons and Fiber:
Unknown. Brads:
Scraparts. Snaps:
Making Memories.
Letter Stamps:
Unknown, Ink: Ranger.
Chipboard: Lil' Davis
Designs
```

Dina Quondamatteo-Berardi is a self-described "lifelong entrepreneur," having opened her first business at the ripe old age of nineteen. After tying the knot in 1998, she started making scrapbooks as a way to organize her wedding and honeymoon pictures. It became an addiction, and in November 2004 she turned her passion for preserving memories into a business, opening the American Scrapbooking Center in Bayside, New York. Just four months later, she co-founded a scrapbook-paper manufacturing company called ZSIAGE, "The Essence of Fabulous," which debuted in July 2005. Quondamatteo-Berardi is married to a fabulous, patient, and saintly man named Anthony and has two-year-old twin babies, Lauren and Antonio.

"YOU HAVE SUCH LOVELY EYES"

pretty girl

Every girl has her pretty parts
-r.d.

PRETTY PARTS

TIPS AND TECH

I used a closeup shot and added a hairpiece embellishment using tulle, ribbon, and a rhinestone.

SUPPLIES

KI Memories paper. Faded Gray paper, Making Memories Page Pebble, Offray Ribbon. Staples, Tulle. String, Rhinestones.

PRETTY GIRL

MOTIVATION

I cut up pieces of a photo (that I'd actually had taken in my garage) and arranged them across the page in a way that I felt highlighted each body part. I felt the separation of the images drew attention to each one's unique beauty.

SUPPLIES

KI Memories paper. Bazzill Basics paper. Offray patterned ribbon, Hancock's stock ribbon, Making Memories Frame, Ribbon rosette, StazOn ink, Tulle fabric.

BETTY SWEETHEART

MOTIVATION

I made up a character, Betty Sweetheart, to showcase the dissatisfaction some women may feel with the role they are given as sweet, polite, and predictable. As a mild-mannered florist she is shown with a distant stare, sitting with her hands folded in her lap. The second page has her as a hot crime fighter, in the vein of *Charlie's Angels*. I wanted to show that a girl can be strong and powerful without giving up her feminine charms. I loved the idea of using her as a character who wasn't satisfied with her job and had an alter ego after 5:00p.m.

TIPS AND TECH

I cut out these poses and used the leftover picture as a stencil. I spray-painted her silhouette onto paint chips to add depth and to emphasize her *Charlie's Angels*-style pose.

SUPPLIES
Doily, Paint chips, Faded Gray paper, Bazzill paper, Spray-paint, Staples, Offray Ribbon, Rhinestones.

208   208
Wild Ca   081

Betty
didn't
like
her
day
job.

Pink Balloon   92082

Fawn Lily   92083

Rachel Denbow is a creative soul who loves to play with fabric, photos, and found objects. She enjoys spreading Fair Trade Awareness in Middle America and can't get enough of Chinese food. She wants to do a hundred things in her life-time, including teach art, design clothes, and own a concert venue. She and her best friend, Elsie, are partners in Red Velvet Art, a line of beautiful handmade products for girls. Denbow is married to a beauti-ful man who inspires and sup-ports her artistic endeavors. She currently lives in Oklahoma but will soon call the Great Northwest her home.

They gave me my curly hair, my first and second car, and my sweet tooth. My meemaw married a WWII soldier that she met @ an army supply store. She loves him so much still. My grandmother churned butter and married the handsome grocer that stocked it. 50 years strong they are.

My story, my opportunity, MY MOMENTS, My Adventure, MY Breath, my mission, MY journey, MY Window, MY YEARS, MY Time, my life.

Joycie May

Dotty.

Rachel

THEY GAVE ME CURLY HAIR

MOTIVATION

My grandmothers' younger days intrigue me. Black and white photos from another era romanticize their stories and make me wish I could have known them when they were my age. Our lives are so connected, and this page is a tribute to the ways they have given to me. Knowing them helps me to know myself.

TIPS AND TECH

I used masking tape and neutral colors to give it a vintage feel.

SUPPLIES

Uighur text on scrap paper, Masking tape, Vintage ribbon, Vintage family photos, Notebook paper. Hindi Bible scanned and printed, Vellum, Lace.

ARTISTS Rachel Denbow and Elsie Flannigan for Red Velvet Art

You who are young, make the most of your youth...follow the impulses of your heart. If something looks good to you, pursue it. But know also that not just anything goes, you have to answer to God for every last bit of it.
ecclesiastes 11:9 The Message

be a brave little girl!

Everyone needs a big field to practice their twirlin!

I have to make myself face my fears of not having what it takes to get to the other side.

BRAVE LITTLE GIRL

SUPPLIES

Pen: Sakura. Other: masking tape, vellum,
dried flowers, paint.

ARTIST: Elsie Flannigan for Red Velvet Art

Red Velvet Art

Red Velvet Art is being little girls. Wearing pink. Having adventures and playing with color. It's for girls who have been told that they need to grow up. Be sensible. We are all a beautiful mess. Red Velvet Art is Elsie Flannigan and Rachel Denbow. Red Velvet Art is a company that although only in its infancy, is bringing beautiful crafts, fashion, and art to the world at large. To experience Red Velvet Art, log on to www.redvelvetart.com.

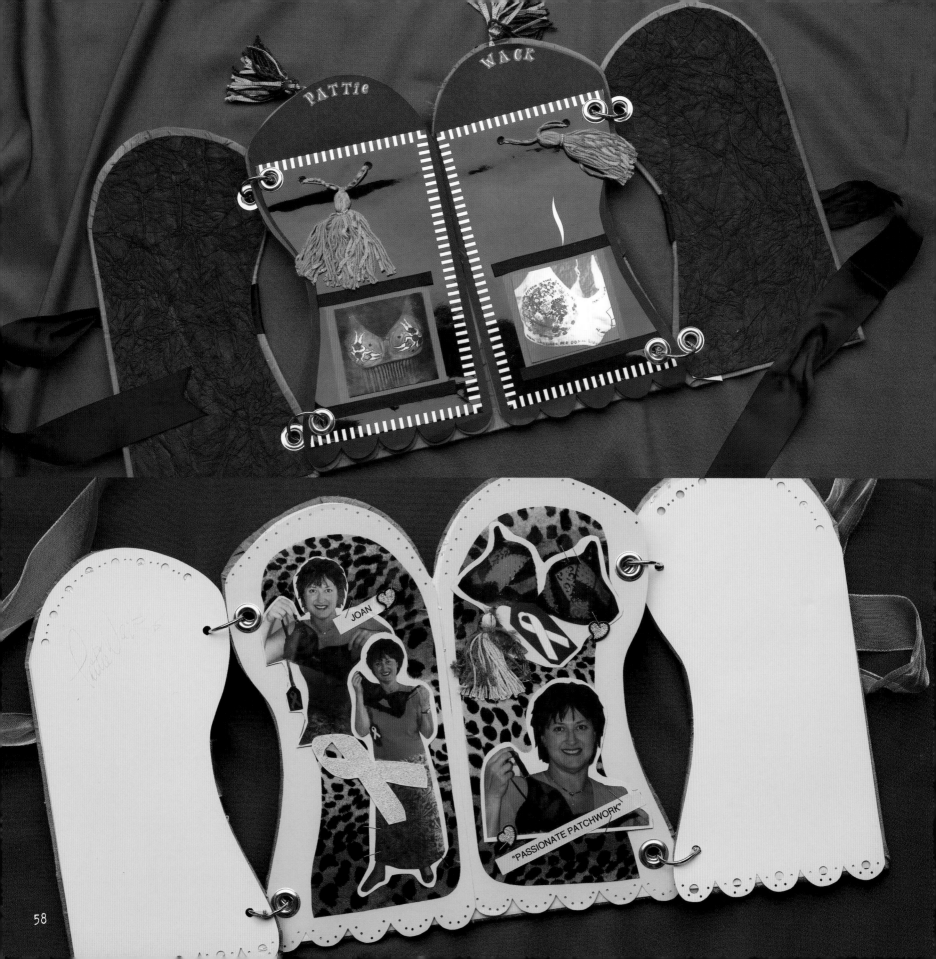

BOSOM BUDDIES

MOTIVATION

Inspired by The Way to Women's Wellness Foundation ArtBra Calendar 2005. (For more information: www.wtww.org)

TIPS AND TECH

Steps for Front and Back Covers:
1. Trace pattern onto cardboard and cut out back cover and two fronts.
2. Lay the three cut-out pieces onto fabric. Trace around. Cut out fabric 1-inch larger around all sides of the traced lines.
3. Spray the wrong side of the fabric pieces with spray adhesive. Lay the cardboard cutouts onto adhesive. Clip the curves with scissors, and

pull the fabric over the cardboard to cover the edges.
4. Cut 1 yard of ribbon in half. Glue the end of the ribbons to the uncovered side of the two front covers, in the curved "waist" of the corset. This will create a closure for the scrapbook.
5. Trace around covered pieces onto scrapbook paper. Cut $1/4$" smaller than the tracing marks. Glue paper cut-outs to the uncovered side of the back and front covers. When gluing the paper onto the front covers, it will hide the glued ends of the ribbon.
6. Apply eight grommets where the pattern indicates, using a grommet application kit.
7. Assemble the front covers to the back cover, using four-ring binders.

Steps for Pages
1. Trace the pattern onto scrapbook paper and cut out for scrapbook pages. Cut scallops on the bottom of the pages to look like lingerie.
2. Punch holes and apply

grommets where the pattern indicates, using a grommet application kit. Punch holes around the top and bottom to create a lace effect.
3. For the "Joan" Page: Cut animal-print paper 1-inch smaller than the pattern and adhere it to the scrapbook pages with clear, tacky glue. Cut out images in photos adhere them to additional paper, and cut out with a $1/2$" border. Adhere photos to the pages and add heart appliqués. Rubber stamp the Awareness stamp to scrapbook paper, and apply beads while the stamp is wet. Let dry, cut out, and adhere to the page. Add a PattieWack tassel and use a stapler to accent the page.
4. For the "Be Smart" Page: Cut four polka dot paper squares of scrapbook paper. Cut two smaller squares of vellum paper, and attach them to two of the polka-dot squares with mini brads at the corners to create pockets. Adhere the pockets to the tops of the pages. Add PattieWack tassels and photos, and rubber stamp "Be Smart" to two tags. Insert the tags into the pockets. Cut two strips of vellum paper and attach to the other

two polka-dot squares with mini brads. Adhere the squares to the bottom of the pages. Slip photos behind the vellum strips, and embellish the page with alphabet brads and hearts.

5. For the "Pattie Wack" Page: Cut black and white striped paper into ½" strips. Adhere to the page as shown in the photo. Punch two holes in the pages, thread PattieWack tassels through the holes and, tie them or tape on the back of the page. Adhere photos to contrasting paper and glue to the page, outlining with black grosgrain ribbon. Add alphabet stickers to the top of the page.

7. Assemble the scrapbook by placing the pages on top of the back cover (face up) and the front covers on top. Insert the ring binders through the grommets, and snap the rings closed. Tie the ribbon in a bow to close the scrapbook.

SUPPLIES

Front and Back Covers:
Heavy Cardboard or Foam Board (2 pieces, 12" x 12"), Silk Fabric of your choice (26" x 13"), Handmade Scrapbook Paper by Provo Craft , Krylon Spray Adhesive (All-Purpose 7010), Grommet Application Kit: 8 ³/₈" Brass Grommets, 4 Brass Ring Binders, 1 Yard of 1½" Ribbon of your choice, Aleene's Clear Gel Tacky Glue, Marker, Hammer Scissors, Pattern for Corset Shape.

Inside Pages
"Joan" Page:
PattieWack Tassel, Scrapbook Paper by Provo Craft , Tulip Awareness Ribbon Stamp Kit (for beaded pink ribbon), Animal Print Gift-Wrap Paper, Aleene's Clear Gel Tacky Glue, Tulip Fashion Frills Heart Appliqués

"Be Smart" Page:
PattieWack Tassel, Scrapbook Paper by Provo Craft , Fiskars Hole Punch, Colorbok Concho Brad Alphabet, Making Memories Mini Brads.

"Pattie Wack" Page:
PattieWack Tassel, Scrapbook Paper by Provo Craft, Alphabitties Alphabet Stickers.

General Supplies:
Krylon Paper Finishes Acid-Free Spray Adhesive, Art Accentz' ¼" Terrifically Tacky Tape, Provo Craft Hole Punches, Provo Craft , Scallop Scissors, Grommet Application Kit, ³/₈" Brass Grommets.

CIRQUE DU CELEBRATION

MOTIVATION

The Teatro ZinZanni Dinner Theatre in Seattle was the locational inspiration for this scrapbook, celebrating the 50th Anniversary of Chuck & Shirley Wilkinson. (For more information: www.zinzanni.org)

TIPS AND TECH

1. Trace mask pattern onto cardboard and cut out.
2. Adhere patchwork of paper to both masks with spray adhesive, folding over the sides to cover the edges.
3. Glue beads to the eye area, and embellish with stickers and cut-outs.
4. Adhere the eyelash rope trim around the edge of the front cover with double-sided tape.
5. Cut out multiple pages for the scrapbook, using the mask pattern.
6. Punch $\frac{1}{4}$" holes in the left corner of the mask covers and in each page. Bind together with the $\frac{1}{4}$" screw post, by pushing the post through the covers and the pages, and insert the screw tightly.
7. Create a tassel using the PattieWack Tassel tool, with fibers/yarn. The top of the tassel on this scrapbook is two tiny plastic cups, covered with beads and glued together! Tie the tassel around the top of the post. Tie several fibers around the post to embellish.
8. Glue a clear cabochon to the top of the post with heavy-duty glue.
9. Glue photos of the event and cut-outs from the dinner program inside the pages. Add alphabet stickers throughout the scrapbook to describe people and content.

SUPPLIES

PattieWack Tassels. Adornaments Fibers/Yarn. Cut-outs from the Teatro ZinZanni Program. Scrapbook Paper: Paper Passport by Provo Craft. One Pound Plus (Brights) by Provo Craft. Paper Symphony (Block II) by Provo Craft. Krylon Spray Adhesive (All-Purpose 7010). Terrifically Tacky Tape ($\frac{1}{4}$" Doublesided). Provo Craft Alphabet Stickers. Provo Craft Alphabitties Stickers. $\frac{1}{4}$" Fiskars Hole Punch. $\frac{1}{4}$" Screw Post. 1 Clear Cabochon. Assorted Beads. 6000 Heavy-Duty Glue.

As a designer, television host, product consultant, and author, Pattie Donham has been crafting everyday things into extraordinary art for more than twenty years. Known by her friends and fans as "Pattie Wack," she is as wacky, disarming, and kind as she seems on her current public-broadcast television show, *Craft Studios*. Her talents range from scrapbooking and sewing to fiber crafts and floral design. In addition to contributing to numerous books and magazines, Donham has appeared on national TV on *The DIY Jewelry-Making Show*, *Aleene's Creative Living*, *Home Matters*, *Our Home*, *QVC Home Shopping*, *Home and Family*, and *The Home Shopping Network*. She also enjoys working on www.pattiewack.com and www.crafttv.net and writing the PattieWack Newsletter.

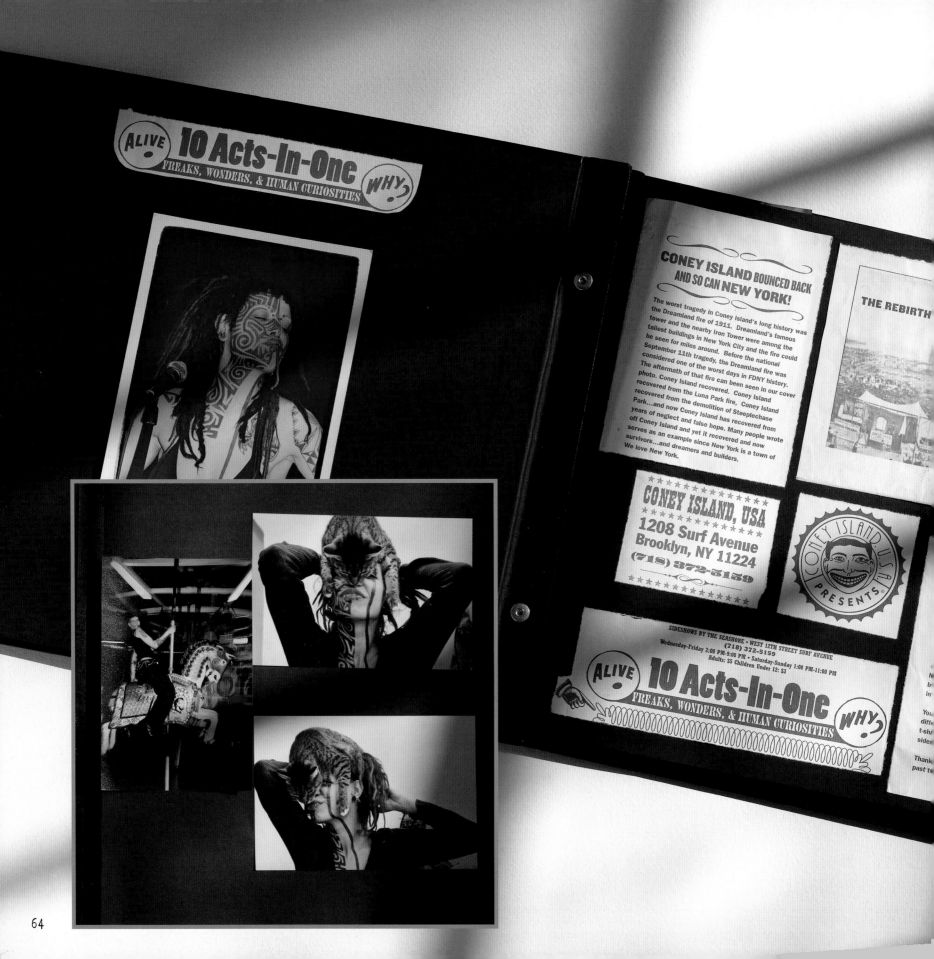

ALIVE 10 Acts-In-One
FREAKS, WONDERS, & HUMAN CURIOSITIES **WHY?**

CONEY ISLAND BOUNCED BACK AND SO CAN NEW YORK!

The worst tragedy in Coney Island's long history was the Dreamland fire of 1911. Dreamland's famous tower and the nearby Iron Tower were among the tallest buildings in New York City and the fire could be seen for miles around. Before the national September 11th tragedy, the Dreamland fire was considered one of the worst days in FDNY history. The aftermath of that fire can be seen in our cover photo. Coney Island recovered. Coney Island recovered from the Luna Park fire, Coney Island recovered from the demolition of Steeplechase Park...and now Coney Island has recovered from years of neglect and false hope. Many people wrote off Coney Island and yet it recovered and now serves as an example since New York is a town of survivors...and dreamers and builders. We love New York.

THE REBIRTH

★★★★★★★★★★
CONEY ISLAND, USA
★★★★★★★★★★
1208 Surf Avenue
Brooklyn, NY 11224
(718) 372-5159
★★★★★★★★★★

SIDESHOWS BY THE SEASHORE • WEST 12TH STREET SURF AVENUE
(718) 372-5159
Wednesday-Friday 2:00 PM-9:00 PM • Saturday-Sunday 1:00 PM-11:00 PM
Adults: $5 Children Under 12: $3

ALIVE 10 Acts-In-One
FREAKS, WONDERS, & HUMAN CURIOSITIES **WHY?**

I WAS born in Brooklyn, NY. However, I grew up all over Suffolk county, NY. After high school graduation I spent a few years in Manhattan & developed some bad habits. I then moved to Minneapolis, MN to escape the negative influences in my life. It was there I found my love for the performing arts. Apocalypse Theatre, a band founded by V & Hope gave me my first taste. I toured with them doin a little bit of back-up vocals and a lot of performance during their set. ~~Eventually~~ V then grew an interest in film & video & I got to be a character in one of his first projects. I had so much fun with those guys. Also during my time in Minnesota, I met the know Nothing Cirkus & I ran away & performed with them. It was a very ~~brief~~ brief stint, but a memorable one none the less. Travelling with a bunch of clowns — Ed the Clown, Stix the Clown & Nostril Dumbass in the back of Johnny Ferrals truck is pretty hard to forget. I re-joined Apox when we got to Burning Man.

Eventually, I made my way back to New York. I was gone so long, there was so much change, & it wasn't the city I used to know & then a week later the World Trade Centre tragedy took place & it was such a sad & scary time. After several months I arranged to move back to Minneapolis. About two or three days before I was suppose to leave I was kidnapped by the World Famous Coney Island Sideshow by the Seashore, so I never did make it back to Minnesota. Dick Zigun initially hired me because of my look. He thought it was funny that I tattooed my face & hands before the rest of me was filled up. I started out eating all these icky, creepy, crawly, squirmy, wormy bugs & started toughening the bottoms of my feet because I wanted to do the ladder of swords act. Also over the course of my time there I ~~ma~~ master ed the skill of fire eating. Sahar taught me the basics of it a couple of years ago, & I'd dabble with it here & there. Then when Tyler Fyre put in his notice that he was leaving to work with the Bros. Grimn Sideshow, I ~~practiced~~ in my room every day for a week & put together a little routine. Then I marched right up Dick & told him I wanted to be the next fire eater!

Mr. Zigun said, well alright, let's see what ya got. Needless to say, INSECTAVORA is now the Coney Island Sideshow Fire Eater.

My performing with the Coney Island Sideshow has definately been the catalyst behind my starting this scrap book.* Once I started performing there I knew I had to document this era of my life however long or short it may be. I'm in my fourth season now & still adding more photos, fliers & every 'scrap in the city' with the name INSECTAVORA on it.

* I'm just so honored to have a place in the history of such a magical piece of AMERICANA

WEDDED BLISS

1. Create scrapbook layout by layering photos onto decorative paper.
2. Accent with thin ribbon
3. Print words on white paper, cut out, sponge with taupe ink.
4. Place layouts between glass, and follow copper foiling & soldering instructions.
5. Solder decorative corners on front cover.
6. Solder beaded wire onto back cover & on each corner of the inside pages.
7. Place pages together and make marks for jump-ring placement. Solder 6 jump rings on the edge of each cover, making sure the jump rings line up and overlap.
8. Tie jump rings together with ribbons.
9. Weave ribbon through all jump rings for the inside spine. Leave end of ribbon long at the top and attach a charm to it, letting it dangle on the inside like a bookmark.

SUPPLIES

Simply Solder Kit: Beaded wire; Charm & Decorative corners: www.scrapalatte.net; Ribbon: May Arts; Paper: Basic Grey; Ink: Ranger.

SOUL MATES

1. Use pre-cut heart shaped glass, taken from a frame found at the dollar store.
2. Cut cardstock into heart shape, using glass as a pattern.
3. Create scrapbook layout by layering photos and word stickers onto cardstock.
4. Place layout between glass, and follow copper foiling & soldering instructions.
5. Use nickel wire to create scroll at bottom and top edges. Solder in place.
6. String beads onto head pin and create a loop attach to the bottom scroll.
7. String ribbon through top scroll to use as a hanger.

SUPPLIES

Simply Solder Kit: www.scrapalatte.net; Ribbon: May Arts; Cardstock: Bazzil; Word Stickers: Pebbles inc.; Heart Glass: Dollar Store; Wire & Beads: Bead Factory

BABY J

TIPS AND TECH

Baby J
1. Cut rectangles out of cardstock for Rub-On letters & date rec'd stamp.
2. Sponge taupe ink onto blue background cardstock and around edges of rectangles.
3. Create scrapbook layout by layering photos onto cardstock with rectangles.
4. Accent with thin ribbon.
5. Place layouts between glass, and follow copper foiling & soldering instructions.
6. Solder safety pin onto corner of front cover. Tie on charms with ribbon.
7. Solder hinge on the inside-center pages. Cut tops off of mini screws.

Solder each head where holes in hinges are.
8. Place pages together and make marks for jump-ring placement. Solder 1 jumping on the front edge of each cover, making sure the jump rings line up.
9. Tie toggle clasp onto the jump rings with ribbon, making sure ribbon is long enough to connect the toggle together.

Baby Feet
1. Cut glass to fit photos.
2. Place photos between glass, and follow copper foiling & soldering instructions.
3. Solder ribbon charm onto top edge of baby photo & one jump ring onto the bottom edge.
4. Solder 1 jump ring onto the top edge of baby foot prints.

5. String wide ribbon through ribbon charm.
6. String smaller ribbon through jump rings, and tie the two pieces together.

SUPPLIES

Simply Solder Kit hinge, charms & toggle clasp): www.scrapalatte.net; Ribbon: Michaels; Cardstock: Bazzil; Ink-Ranger; Rub-Ons: Making Memories; Date Rec'd Stamp: Office depot; Ribbon: May Arts; Ribbon Charm: Scrappin' Peeps.

Li-sa Blu-hm (n.) 1: Loving wife to Allen 2: Devoted mother to Cameron and Jordan 3: Faithful Christian 4: Owner of Scrap a Latte 5: Instructor specializing in soldered art 6: Also enjoys spending time with family, camping, quadding, exercise, martial arts, having fun, and laughing 7: Resides in Washington State.

(See also)

Ar-tist (n.) 1: one who professes and practices an imaginative art

Cre-ative (n.) 1: one (as an artist or writer) that is creative

Pas-sio-nate (adj.) 1: capable of, affected by, or expressing intense feeling

Orig-i-nal (n.) 1a: a person of fresh initiative or inventive capacity 1b: a unique or eccentric person

kisses xoxoxo love hugs kisses

my SISTER

ses xoxoxo love

kled pink

SISTERS

MOTIVATION

"In my layout, I use a beautiful quote from a good friend and fellow designer: 'The best gift I ever gave my daughter was a sister.' With sisters and daughters I cherish, they are my daily inspiration, and that translates into everything I do and am," says Ann. With three daughters of her own, Karen agrees wholeheartedly.

TIPS AND TECH

On the Cover: Trim 12" x 12" adornment sheet (Fleur Cream) to 8" x 8". Tie Black XOXO ribbon (neutral assortment) around cover chipboard with acrylic paint accents. Use circa foam stamps for title. Print photos on photo canvas.

Pages 1 and 2: background paper — Etcetera pink diamonds and blue scriptina. Use chipboard words "be yourself" and "silly girls" from Dimensional Ephemera pack "Beauty Queen" assortment. Use acrylic paint as accent.

Mount to chipboard tags covered in Etcetera patterned paper. Use Etcetera "Tickled Pink" ribbon to tie tags. Print photos and quotes onto canvas, trim with pinking shears, and mount to black cardstock. Zig Zag stitch using Zision sewing machine.

Stamp using Etcetera diamond background stamp with permanent ink onto transparency sheet. Trim with XOXO ribbon. Use "Sisters" & "Love" chipboard pieces from Dimensional Ephemera Pastel "Words" set.

Use "Enjoy" Epoxy Jemz stickers inside long rectangle bezel; use any stemmed flower as an accent.

Pages 3 and 4: Place diamond-stamped transparency on top of Etcetera blue solid paper. Mat canvas picture with pink scriptina paper, blue diamonds paper, and black cardstock. Use "Silly" ribbon and "Tickled Pink" ribbon.

Use Circa uppercase foam stamps to stamp the word "SISTERS." Accent with "Time Flies" Jemz sticker in rectangle bezel.

Ann Randall Merrill and Karen Randall Lemieux, two lively "thirtyish-somethings" who work together to design a vintage scrapbook line for Provo Craft, embody sisterhood and style. Growing up in a house full of girls, they always cherished the special bond between sisters. But it wasn't until they started scrapbooking their childhood memories that they realized the need for more variety in the industry. "We had so many great photos, but all the vintage embellishments were too dreary," Merrill says. "We wanted something with a vintage look but a fun, youthful feel." And so it was that Etcetera was born. "The name defines abundance," Merrill says. "And that's my mantra in life!"

GETTING PAST THE *PAST* AND THE PAIN

THEN

we had a pretty stormy mother/son relationship

Mom: Pull up your pants. You look like a slob.

Josh: All you ever do is bitch at me.

Mom: Take that stinking cigarette out of your mouth.

Josh: Shut Up!

Mom: You shut up!

Josh: I *hate* you!

Mom: Fine, I *hate* you too!

GETTING PAST THE PAST

MOTIVATION

I made this page after seeing my grown son with his own children and realizing that I had made a lot of mistakes with him. I wanted our relationship to start over again, but this time as two adults instead of adult and child.

Now you are a grown man with two kids of your own. I see how good you are with them and I wonder how you did it with such a lousy role model as a parent.

I accept you for who you are now. I hope you can accept me too.

NOW

TIPS AND TECH

I randomly stamped the background and parts of the journaling boxes by taping off all except for a small strip of a texture stamp. I then inked the exposed part and stamped around the cardstock and journal boxes. The letters for Then and Now were foam letters that I painted with copper metallic paint. The clocks are from Diecuts With a View.

YOUNG and FREE

I want to live my life on my own terms. I want to take my own risks. I want to be allowed to make my own mistakes.

EXHILARATION

YOUNG AND FREE

MOTIVATION

I was inspired to make this page after my youngest son broke both of his wrists while skating. I have always worried about him doing dangerous stunts, but he is old enough to make his own decisions now. Unfortunately, he has also had to suffer the consequences of those decisions.

TIPS AND TECH

Cover: Trim 12" x 12". I made the chipboard tag on the first page by attaching my photo to the chipboard, sanding the edges to distress it, and sealing with Modge Podge. On the second page, I made the "bloody bandage" by tearing some gauze and then staining it with two colors of Ranger Distress inks. The metal photo corner is by Pewter Accents. The blue-jean patterned paper is by Karen Foster.

Nancy McCoy started scrapbooking seven years ago, when her oldest son was expecting his first child. But instead of scrapping her grandkids, she ended up scrapping her relationship with her sons, Joshua and Calvin. "Our relationship is funny, rocky, unique, poignant, semi-dysfunctional, and never politically correct," she says. "I love trying to capture their personalities on paper." McCoy credits her husband, Brad, with being a quiet supporter and part-time critic of her work. "If I try to write some flowery prose on a page, he will give me a look that sends me right back to the scrap room to do it over," she says. In addition to being published in several magazines, McCoy started the TIPsters, one of the first Internet scrapbooking critique groups.

I will not hit bo...

BODY

ART

Carlene Federer

BEAUTIFUL

BRAINY

...ROOKE

I will n...

...no...

...not...

...no...

...not hit bo...

BEING BROOKE

MOTIVATION

Being the mother of a teenage boy, I don't get many opportunities to do "girly" stuff in my scrapbooks – so when my friend Connie dropped by with her daughter Brooke before taking her to a dance, I grabbed Brooke and we did an impromptu photo session! Brooke was a natural model, and I ended up taking two rolls of film. The photos turned out excellent, and I couldn't wait to make some scrapbook pages out of them. Even though I didn't know what I would do with it, I had bought the "I will not hit boys" paper because I thought it was so funny. These photos were the perfect fit for the paper. I added some pink papers and accents, some flowers and labels, and voila! The "Being Brooke" layout was complete!

TIPS AND TECH

Layer pink striped and fabric paper over "I will not hit boys" paper for background. Ink edges of photos with pink stamp pad to distress and make a "border" for the photos. Add to background paper. Randomly add photo corners and frames, and tape to photos. Print out descriptive words with Dymo label maker; add to layout. Add measuring tape along bottom of layout. Use metal "B"s combined with rub-on letters to write "Being Brooke" on the cover of the mini book. Add tickets to cover and ribbons along spine of mini book. Use printed twill for book closure. Add rub-on quote marks, exclamation point, and flowers to finish layout.

SUPPLIES

Patterned Paper: KI Memories, Rusty Pickle. Stamp Pads: Stampin' Up! & Ancient Page. Rub-ons: Autumn Leaves, Stamped & Punctuate. Rub-on Monogram: Me & My Big Ideas. Silver "B"s: Scrap Metal. Chipboard "b": Lil Davis Design. Garter, Printed Twill. Mini Book: 7Gypsies. Flowers: Annalis Scraptique, Prisma, Making Memories. Tape, Chipboard Flower, Photo Corners. Frame & Label Holder: Heidi Swapp. Label Maker: Dymo. Ribbon: Memory Lane, Magic Scraps. Others: Velcro, Staples, Measuring Tape, Rick-Rack, Tickets, Rhinestones.

Carlene Federer was introduced to scrapbooking nearly ten years ago at a neighborhood party, where she was instructed to cut her photos into stars and hearts and to give each photo a (preferably cutesy) caption. "Add in a lot of random stickers, and what do you have? Something definitely not hip," she says. "I shudder to think of what I did to some perfectly innocent photos." Federer kept scrapbooking but quickly learned to ignore everything she'd learned at that party. She now enjoys combining vintage photos with bright colors and modern accents, and she has even begun experimenting with scrapbook-type collages on nontraditional surfaces like cardboard and canvas. "Scrapbooking: It's not just for soccer moms anymore!" she says. Her articles have appeared in *Legacy* magazine, *Creating Keepsakes*, and elsewhere.

The search for mR right.

I blame the movies. Pretty Woman, Dirty Dancing, Sleepless in Seattle. All those romantic movies that end with the girl finding her Mr Right. And while I'm not looking for a Richard Gere, I still would like to meet a nice, handsome, intelligent man to come and simply sweep me off my feet.

There's a quote from Charlotte in one of my favorite Sex and the City episodes - I've been dating since I was 14, where is he? This resonates in my head every so often. There are millions of single men out there. So why is it so hard to meet that perfect one?

I've had four long term relationships. All were wonderful on the best days and horrible on the worst. But with each guy I learned a lot, I learned what I liked and didn't like in a guy. I also discovered a lot about myself - what kind of girlfriend I wanted to be, what I brought to a relationship, and what I need from a partner. Important knowledge to acquire before that trip down the aisle.

So maybe Mr Right isn't in my near future. Maybe I'll have to go through a few more Mr Wrongs before my search is over. But even as the days go by, relationships end, and I suffer through bad first dates, I still keep up hope. I know my tom hanks is out there.

UNCONDITIONAL LOVE

MR. RIGHT

MOTIVATION

I did the layout to remember past relationships and keep my positive attitude for the future.

TIPS AND TECH

Start with scraps of your favorite papers; line them up on the bottom edge of the layout. Cut out the four photos and arrange them in a square. Cut out the circle for the middle and add rubons. Decorate pages with ribbon. Add title and journaling.

SUPPLIES

Paper: KI Memories. Cardstock: Bazzill. Ribbon: KI Memories. Stickers &

Rubons: American Crafts, Doodlebug, and KI Memories. Font: "SP Spence" downloaded from ScrapSupply.com.

Kelly Purkey is not your average scrapper. At twenty-three years old, with no husband, kids, or even cute pets to scrap, her focus is on—you guessed it—Kelly. She's scrapped on and off for five years, but it wasn't until she discovered the great scrapping communities on the Internet that her interest grew to a whole new level. "I've come to cherish my friendships with other scrappers as much as the layouts I create," she says. "I'm always looking for a new technique—and a new friend!" Purkey graduated from Michigan State University with a degree in Media Arts and now works as a photographer (the kind with a video camera at a local news station). She plans to move to New York City to pursue a career in broadcasting.

HALLZIE

MOTIVATION

This page was the day
we put down our family
Rottweiler of 10 years.
She was as much a part
of our family as any of
us. The page is simple
because it didn't need
anything more. There
was too much emotion
going on to squeeze on
the page.

TIPS AND TECH

I used Polaroid MIO photos
taken of her lying in her
favorite place in the yard
before we took her to be
put down. I put them in
these tiny little vellum
envelopes, which allow you
to see what's inside but
still protect it.

Last year, in the middle of July, there was a random day that checked in at just 72 degrees with a breeze—surprising for Atlanta. Tracy Galasso spent it outside with her boyfriend and a bottle of wine, laughing. It later took three pages in her journal to accurately catch the importance of that day. The lesson? "Chronicle the days that matter to you, not just the ones preprinted on your calendar," she says. Galasso, now 26, lives in Atlanta, Georgia, with her boyfriend and dog. She received a BFA in drawing from the Atlanta College of Art. Her days are spent making things with her hands, observing patterns, and trying to be more aware of it all.

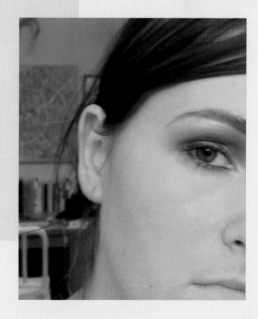

BRAN & JEN

laugh

2005

watching Office Space & Jerry Maguire, drinking lots of vintage champagne & red wine from my cellar, ordering Italian delivery, chattering with our attorneys at 9 pm on a Friday night, toasting the start of our new corporation every other minute, and generally loving life

STICK IT TO THE MAN

friends

DICKY FOX
The key to this job is personal relationships.

As Jerry continues typing, his voice is excited now.

JERRY'S VOICE
And suddenly it was all pretty clear. The answer was fewer clients. Caring for them, caring for ourselves, and the games too. Starting our lives, really.

SHOT OF SENTENCE   We must embrace what is still virginal about our own enthusiasm, we must crack open the tightly clenched fist and give back a little for the common good, we must simply be the best versions of ourselves... that goodness will be unbeatable and the money will appear.

He pauses, and wipes his eyes, still considering the sentence.

STICK IT TO THE MAN

MOTIVATION

In early 2005, a dear friend (and colleague of mine) decided to buy our company. It was either that or be out of a job and also leave a lot of our clients (who we love dearly) stranded without another provider for what we do. Of course, any time you separate from someone or someplace you've been with for a long time, there is always going to be emotion. Ours came to a head one night — happy, sad, angry, confused — over three bottles of champagne/wine and a *Jerry Maguire/Office Space* movie marathon. We kept watching the pivotal job scenes in both movies until we knew most of the words — and at some point during our third bottle, my friend Lesley snapped this impromptu toast. I love this photo because it is so candid you can almost see the motion in the shadow on the wall. It's not entirely flattering, and that's okay.

The reference ("Stick it to the Man"), incidentally, came from a former employee of ours who always felt that we ("The man") were always finding new and improved ways to do her wrong. While they were quite imagined (as were some of our ramblings that night), our drinking and toasting was in defiance of that invisible "man" who always metaphorically holds us all back in our heads. Over the course of the evening, that became our rally cry.

TIPS AND TECH
Journaling
"Watching Office Space & Jerry Maguire, drinking lots of vintage champagne & red wine from my cellar, ordering Italian delivery, chattering with our attorneys at 9 pm on a Friday, toasting the start of our new corporation every other minute, and generally loving life."

TECHNIQUE
Photo was converted to black and white and reprinted. (The blue effect, incidentally, was accidental — I ran it in grayscale rather than true black & white). Print journaling and movie quote onto cardstock. Position patterned paper in strips onto patterned paper base. Add journaling (trimmed), photo, and decorative elements.

A Tip From "The Man": Download a favorite song lyric or movie quote from the Internet. A Google search on a few key words will normally yield lyrics or quotes (or try a website like imdb.com for well-known movie quotes and facts).

SUPPLIES

Patterned Paper: Scrapworks. Cardstock: Bazzill. Computer fonts: Carbon Type. Other: Movie quote (internet—from Jerry Maguire). *Scrapworks* decorative elements (conchos, tabs, rub-ons, cardstock stickers).

While others may not relate to all-night parties in Asian hotel rooms or weekend jaunts to Europe, Jennifer Lynn Moody believes in capturing the moments of her life. "I believe it's necessary to be honest when creating, which means embracing failure and learning to laugh at embarrassing moments," she says. "Too many individuals censor themselves in their albums—they tell less of who they are and more of who they wish they could be." A self-proclaimed Renaissance woman, Moody now serves as chairman of two small corporations and still finds time to travel extensively and cook occasionally for two dozen of her closest friends. She hopes to adopt a child from China during the next few years and have someone to pass her albums on to.

LANDFLAG

MOTIVATION

The inspiration for this book came from a trip I made to Scotland when I was trying to decide whether to return there to live (the process of identifying home as Home, and recognizing the important things for what they really are).

The CD-book format is important, as it is in homage to an artist friend who created a book in a CD for an Edinburgh festival artists bookwork exhibition in 1993. It was on this trip to Scotland that I first saw this incredible art book, which strongly encouraged me to travel the country. I fell in love with the place and ultimately stayed.

TIPS AND TECH

I had rubberstamps made of some of my favorite personal line drawings — all ones connected with personal symbols of travel and the common themes between the landscapes of Scotland and New Zealand. I felt more comfortable using my own imagery, since it was both personal to me, yet one step removed from the raw process of drawing. This way I could be more objective about the results. I drew the basic outlines on mount-board squares cut to fit inside the CD box. The rough drawings were based on sketches made 10 years ago on a trip to Scotland.

I used Stewart Gill Colourise acrylic paints (Kingfisher, Ochre, Cerise, Plum, White, Olive, Lemon) and Caran d'ache watercolor crayons to color up the backgrounds, then rubber stamped in black crafter's ink. The surface was further worked into with Stewart Gill Fresco Flakes (Alabaster) and tailor's interlining to create texture.

Additional scripted pieces were glued on, and letraset wording added. The cover was quilters' cotton (quilting has everything in common with scrapbooking!) stamped, painted and stitched.

The internal extra book consists of acetate pages of my stamped designs and some text (about the notions of traveling and home) and watercolor paper that has been stamped and painted. Small paper rivets hold the acetate sections on. I like transparent sections in scrapbooking — they serve as reminders that our life experience at any given moment is a multi layered stack of resonating sounds, sights, and feelings, that somehow manage to occupy the same physical space. I don't see the need for text to be readable necessarily — it's part of the visual experience, and words are not always enough.

Rebecca Gill

Rebecca Gill has been making collage-style scrapbooks since she first emigrated from Scotland to New Zealand at the age of eleven. She has since traveled extensively, which has inspired her artwork to explore issues connected with landscape identification, the notions of home and belonging, and insider/outsider status. "Immigrants often have a fragmented personal history," she says, "and the need to 'create or fabricate' a cohesive personal memory can be vitally important in restructuring a fractured sense of identity or belonging." Now living back in Scotland with her husband and three-year-old son, Gill is the creative director of Stewart Gill Ltd., a manufacturer of high-performance art and craft products

DANCE
like noone is watching

STAS AT SEATTLE
DOM POLSKI 1/2005

DANCE

MOTIVATION

To emphasize motion and lack
of self-consciousness in my
toddler.

TIPS AND TECH

Journaling
"Dance like no one is watching."

I blended the photos with
custom designed papers created from velvet-like colors
and photographic remnants.

SUPPLIES

Software: Digitally scrapped
in Adobe Photoshop 7. Fonts:
Dirty Ego;Porcelain from
www.misprintedtype.com.
Photos: David J. Gunkel.

* Paper and embellishments
by the artist for: design
butcher (Café Sorbet
Collection, Coffee Talk
Collection Grade A Scraps
Vol. 2 CD Rom)

Ann Hetzel Gunkel, a dedicated "crafts hater," curiously finds herself the founder and head designer of www.designbutch-er.com, a digital scrapbooking firm. Her foray into the field began when her multimedia creations collided with her passion for documenting her spectacular toddler son. She now she considers her work to be "scrapping with an urban edge." A feminist scholar, she is also intrigued by the meaning of "women's arts and crafts": scrapbooking began in the Victorian age as a way to keep homebound "proper" women busy, and Hetzel Gunkel loves turning that intention on its head. A product designer for Scrap Girls, she lives happily ever after with her family in a Chicago bungalow. She can be reached at info@designbutcher.com.

[ANCIENT GREEK: TO STAND OUTSIDE ONESELF]

[EK-STASIS]

holiday 2004

THE POINT IS TO PLUNGE
INTO IT TO THE
POINT OF ECSTASY.
THAT IS WHAT HOLIDAYS
ARE FOR.

-JEAN BEAUDRILLARD

ECSTATIC

MOTIVATION

As a professor of cultural studies (Ph.D. in postmodern philosophy), I tend to create layouts that reflect metaphysical concepts. In this case, I draw on the text of French postmodernist Jean Beaudrillard. Because the journaling presents the root word for ecstasy (standing outside oneself).

TIPS AND TECH

Journaling
"The point is to plunge into it to the point of ecstasy. That is what holidays are for." Jean Beaudrillard; "Ekstasis: Ancient Greek: To stand outside oneself."

TECHNIQUE
I wanted the photo techniques to reflect the notion of separation. Thus, I desaturated and digitally chopped the right-hand photo to emphasize the movement and laughter. For the left hand focal photo, I created a "digital packing tape transfer" to add visual interest.

SUPPLIES

Software: Digitally scrapped in Adobe Photoshop 7
Fonts: Misproject downloaded from www.misprintedtype.com; Jet plane; Virginia Plain
Photos: David J. Gunkel

* Supplies: Striped paper, holiday music paper, tags, and index tabs created by the artist for design butcher's Candy Cane Lane Collection (Grade A Scraps Volume 1 CD Rom)

LIFE IN THE BOX

MOTIVATION

Tired of carting around a grandma purse full of scraps and whatnot that help you make it through life? Simplify! Create this Life in a Box to easily keep track of where you need to be, how you need to get there and why you need to go.

(ticket stubs, receipts). Inside the internal nesting box, stash your get up and go gear. It is a good idea to keep your internal box small so that the outer boxes remain portable. Travel light — a cell phone/PDA, some change, id and debit cards — that's all you need.

Bernadette Henderson

TIPS AND TECH

On the Cover: Trim 12" x 12" Categorize your pile of scraps and use them to decorate a set of nesting boxes. For this project, I divided my scraps into resourceful bits (schedules, calendars), get up and go bits (ads for restaurants, places to see), directions (maps, maps and more maps) and actual scraps

Born and raised in El Paso, Texas, Bernadette Henderson is a freelance artist/photographer/writer trapped in the body of a higher education administrator. Granting access to college by day, by night she writes diversity columns for the local paper, photographs the Pacific Northwest, and scraps the most random aspects of life that others would never think to ponder. Henderson generally creates works on commission for friends of friends of friends who are in the market for "something different" with which to start conversations in their homes. Purposefully affordable, highly individualized, and exquisitely detailed, her non-traditional coffee table books never fail to inspire and spark curiosity.

the H

desk guide to the Avoidable Journey

...AT A MACY'S DAY AFTER THANKSGIVING SALE W/O MY BOYFRIEND'S PLATINUM CARD...

CREDIT ◆
1234 5678 9012 3456
RICH SPENDER

...SITTING FIRST CHAIR TRYING TO SQUEAK OUT A HIGH C#...

1ST CHAIR CLARINET

...AT THE END OF TIME...

...TAKING A STROLL DOWN LOVER'S LANE...

love love love love

...AGAIN...

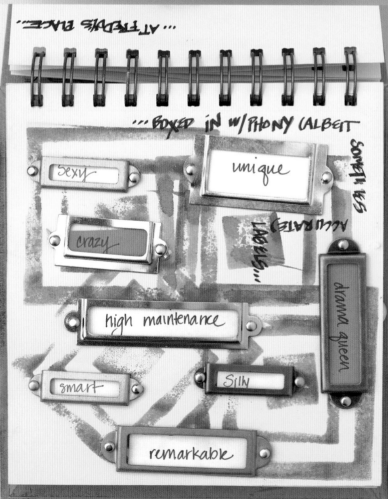

...BOXED IN W/ PHONY CALBEIT

sexy

unique

crazy

high maintenance

drama queen

smart

silly

remarkable

THE H DESK GUIDE TO THE AVOIDABLE JOURNEY

MOTIVATION

Why are there no travel/life guides out there to tell you where not to go and what not to do? In the grand scheme of all gals who can never say no, this guide spells out a few of the very big no-no's from Ms. H's desk. From buying a car without a guy to shopping at Macy's without your boyfriend's credit card, this fun guide alerts the Just Say Yes girl to just when she really needs to Just Say No.

TIPS AND TECH

With a lot of non-matching ideas, you can go for consistency of look by using one product throughout the book. To tie this book together, I used Fiber Scraps TintZ (in a variety of colors including Denim, Stone, Rose, Walnut Ink and Tea Stain) to do the stamping on each page of this book.

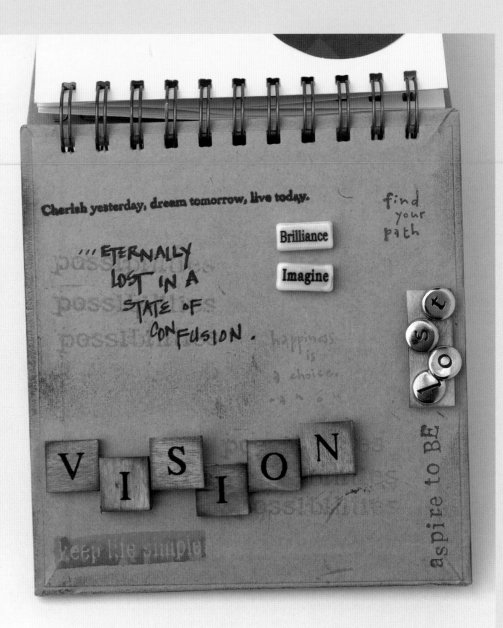

ANGELS

MOTIVATION

I find my inspiration in a variety of places, but mostly in the beauty and grace of women. I am a lesbian, and I have always been very attracted to the softness of other women. My brother Jac Ever, with whom I live, is a painter, and his influence of color upon me is very strong. I am very interested in angels, and I like them to be represented in my work. I also find much inspiration in the poems of Pablo Neruda and the tranquility of the countryside where I live.

Estelle was born in Paris in July of 1975. She has studied at the National School of Decorative Arts of Paris — Section photographs. Since 1998 she has worked with her brother Jac Ever — decorator of spectacle. His work has been seen on French television and at the Lido of Paris.

After a road accident and a handicap (deafness), she presently devotes herself to working with the the digital image. Her principal source of inspiration comes from the power and grace of women. She continues her quest to develop art that reflects a softness and beauty that can only be found in an oneiric world. Estelle lives and works in the Dordogne, France.

maxwell

PEOPLE FROM THE CITY

MOTIVATION

I started this piece by going on an adventure in downtown San Diego. I knew I wanted to do some small portraits, so I simply walked down Broadway looking at faces. As I was walking, I would pick out the most interesting people and try to get a good long stare at their facial expressions.

While walking I would pick up little pieces of paper and trash, then put them into my backpack and continue on. Sometimes the best supplies are free, blowing down the street.

When I got home that night, I emptied everything from my pack onto the floor of my room and started to draw the people I'd seen downtown from memory. I culled all of my inspiration and most of my supplies from the city itself so that my end result would be a product of the city and the scraps you find there.

TIPS AND TECH

Begin by drawing small portraits on scraps of paper you have lying around the house. The next step is setting "the stage" so to speak. Find a strong piece of paper. This is the area where you will begin collaging elements of line, color, and texture together to house the small portraits you've drawn.

After everything is in place, coat it all with dirty water and coffee.

SUPPLIES

Glue stick, pens, scraps of papers and trash... and a cup of coffee.

Maxwell Holyoke-Hirsch was born in San Diego, California. As a small boy, he spent most of his time drawing, banging on pots and pans, and playing television tag. "Now I'm working on my illustration portfolio," he says. "I fill the time in-between by drinking a lot of coffee, staying up late, and drawing and photographing the people I meet and the places I go—capturing moments and revisiting them in the form of art."

•New LeASh & CoLLAr•

this is all part of a plot I have to introduce my kitties to the outside world so they can play in our back yard in the spring. 2.27.2005

the big bad world was clearly quite overwhelming for Charlie Strokes, Esq. on his first time out. He spent the whole walk in the crouch position, yelling at the sky.

welcome little cat

Welcome to the world.

THE FIRST WALK OF MR. CHARLIE STROKES, ESQ.

Dawn Mordaski

MOTIVATION

To document the first walk of my cat, Mr. Charlie Strokes, Esq.

TIPS AND TECH

There are five journaling tags on this page. They are all decorated in slightly different but coordinating ways, using the same stamps, colors, and papers to create simultaneous effects of rhythm and interest. Three are handwritten journaling bits, and two are larger, stamped messages.

TECHNIQUE

All the cardstock I used on this page is solid-colored, from an economy-sized pack of cardstock from Wal-Mart. To create the red textured background, I used a magenta-colored ink pad and my natural-colored Magic Mesh (which is cheaper than the colored ones). I laid the Magic Mesh down on the page and did direct-to-paper-inking over various spots, using different amounts of pressure to achieve varying degrees of intensity. That gives the red background sheet its texture and simultaneously dyes my Magic Mesh the perfect shade to use on this page.

To create the large pink and orange vertical stripes, I used solid papers and Stampin' Up's Petal Prints stamp set, along with three shades of red and pink ink. I stamped the blank papers randomly with the flower stamps, starting with the largest shapes and working my way to the smallest. On the orange page I also used the rectangular stamp from the same set, for a bit of angle flavor. After I stamped the pages and gave them a moment to dry, I tore them into strips, which I then placed in a stripe pattern on the red page.

I matted the two focal photos on black paper, leaving them in their original rectangular shape. The other photos I cropped by tearing. Then I inked the edges of my torn photos, to make them "pop" and to maintain the pleasing visual continuity of having all the layout's photos outlined black in one way or another.

The tags are stamped and the edges inked, similar to the title pieces. Using the same ribbon on all the different tags also creates rhythm and adds texture. The beads and wire woven through the small "Mr. Guy" tag and the word "Charlie" do the same thing — though they add a different sort of texture, creating a more visually stimulating page — more to look at!

I used regular old office staples to adhere some of the pieces of the page — partly just to add visual interest, and partly to echo the metal of the leash in the photos. The titles are stamped using Stampin' Up's Newsprint Alphabet and Paint Prints sets. I varied the shapes of my title pieces for visual interest — some are torn, some are tags, and some are tiles (created by stamping letters onto the pink paper also used in the background, and then placing transparent tiles from StickO over the letters, and cutting them out). By choosing to create the title pieces to echo the shapes, colors and other elements that occur throughout the layout, you create rhythm, which draws the eye through the page, allowing the viewer to find cohesion in the lovely chaos.

HOMEGROWN

A man was killed on a warm friday night in May. His name was Johnny Blaze. He was twenty-three, 6 foot two, brown (eyes twinkling) and brown (hair curling around his ears). He was (loving, loyal) husband to Yvette, (adoring, doting) father to Dalilah, Starfania, and Skylynn. He was the laughingest man I ever knew.

There are no remaining photographs of Johnny Blaze. The few I took one afternoon in his apartment, of him dancing and hamming with his little girls, they got lost in the shuffle. I think Danielle took them when we both moved out of our apartment, when she went to rehab and I went to my mom's to breathe, regroup, sleep, mend. This is what I have this bleak green and brown photo of the place where he died. This is all I have left of the man who taught me to play dominos, the man who could make me crack up laughing with just one eyebrow. He had three daughters, he had a wife who loved him. A disabled mother in law who depended on the income he brought in.

This is where and how Johnny was raised. He finished high school, an obstacle conquered. He'd already been selling drugs since he was fourteen. It was a career here, than for a smart quick boy with ambition. You were chosen, trained, you earned money and respect quicker than a soldier. Williamsburg, Brooklyn, 1999. There weren't many other business opportunities open to Johnny. And so his daughters had clothes, they had food, birthday parties, mango ice from the icey man and friday night dinners with the whole familia giggling and having pillow-fights with their cousins. Johnny's daughters got to see him dance with their mother, how they were one heart beating between four eyes, how we could all see love there in the room between them.

Johnny Blaze was killed for eight hundred dollars he owed on the street. He was beaten to death with a baseball bat by a gang of boys hired by the man to whom he owed the money. Several of the men held his wife, Yvette, and forced her to watch him die. I'm saying they made her watch him bleed and crumple, and he screamed but didn't beg, and the police said they had nothing to go on and there was no obituary. But the service at the church was packed.

Now my life is far away from that time and place, but I miss Johnny every day, and I know I'm not the only one.

HOMEGROWN

MOTIVATION

To remember the tragic loss of a friend.

TIPS AND TECH

The black, rust, and sage background papers are from Basic Grey, Black Tie Collection. The "Homegrown," "Legacy," and "Love" Labels are stickers from Pebbles, inc. To make "Homegrown" stand out as the title, I double-matted it, using Kraft paper, and paper printed with an old map, from K&Company, the Life's Journey Series (this paper also appears on several of the journaling tags).

The rub-on "Old Friend," which is in the bottom-left corner of the large photo, is from ProvoCraft.

The tag in the bottom right-hand corner that reads "More precious than Gold" is a copper gift tag from a company called Garden Walk. I bought them at the Container Store, in a pack of 5 for $5.99. They come with ribbon ties and are extremely easy to use—you just write on them with a ballpoint pen or a pencil, and you can either emboss them or deboss them. The metal is extremely malleable, but also would hold up to distressing and painting and all sorts of creative action.

On the journaling tags: the manila-colored tags are from Avery. The Kraft paper on which most of the journaling tags are printed comes from Stampin' Up. The antique brads and the black gingham ribbon are also from Stampin' Up; the solid black ribbon is from Making Memories. The rust colored fibers are from EK Success. Each tag is printed with its own font, as is the large journaling block on the first page. All of them are downloaded from the wonderfully easy-to-use and free site fontfreak.com.

I printed the large journaling block on a transparency from Staples, which I then laid over the sage-colored, distressed-patterned paper. Because the journaling was difficult to write, and because I really wanted to work on making it say what I wanted it to, I started the journaling weeks before I began laying out the page. Even that's a bit of a lie. This is one of those pages I have known I needed to make since I began scrapping. So I've been working on the journaling in my head since then, kind of. At least in the way that your mind works through things slowly first, without words. Anyway, keeping the journaling saved as a Word file on my computer, and working on it slowly over a few weeks, adding to it, trying different voices and fonts and styles – all of that helped me to feel satisfied with what I ultimately wrote.

Because the only photo I have left is the one of the space where Johnny died, I had it blown up to 8 x 10. I then trimmed its edges with a deckle scissor, and used the same scissor to cut a thin black matte for the photo, to help it stand out on the page. I used black antique brads to fasten the photo to the page on only three sides, creating a pocket for the journaling tags.

In a good scrapbook page, as in a good poem, every single element has meaning. The colors chosen for this layout each echo bits of the event — black for night, green for money, red for blood. The paper has been distressed. The gingham ribbon on the tags about the little girls is meant to evoke the traditional associations of little girls with such fabrics; the rusty fibers echo the shade of SkyLynn's hair. I chose

some old coins I found lying around the house to bring the money element into the page in a really visual way. The one in the center has No Cash Value and is emblazoned with a Bald-Eagle-and-Stars crest. I used the map paper to matte the title and some of the journaling because for me, this person's life and death are both really tied to place. Johnny was a Puerto Rican man from Brooklyn. He was a boy of the streets becoming a man of the streets, and he died for it. Among other things, the maps symbolize Johnny's relationship to his place,

his city, his language, his country. And they symbolize how far away he's gone now.

THE PHOTOS
Camera: my old 35mm Minolta. Film: Fuji, 400 speed.

I shot this photo at around 8:00 on a Saturday morning in the early spring of 2004.

Dawn Mordaski is a voracious reader, big sister to five amazing teenagers, and proud mother of two stunningly gorgeous cats, Lily Pad Thai and Charlie Strokes, Esq. She has spent most of her life studying various items of interest, including spoken-word poetry, transgressive teaching techniques, Mary Magdalene, oral history, children's literature, queer theory, and social activism—and she insists that her desire to scrap is connected with all of them. For her, scrapping is about telling a story the only way you can—finding the truth for yourself and not depending on anyone else to create it for you. In addition to owning the New York City–based custom-scrapbooking company DreamBooks, Mordaski is now at work on a novel called Her Angel.

i never...

...have taken **psychedelic** drugs of any kind. Must've been the after-school special where the girl jumped out the window while **tripping** on angel dust. And then when William Hurt regressed into an ape in Altered States it kinda ruined the whole isolation tank thing for me.

Call me a **scaredy-cat** if you will, but I prefer to place my mind enhancing experiences into the hands of the three wise men: Jim Beam, Jack Daniels, and **José Cuervo**. ¡Mas tequila!

I NEVER

MOTIVATION

I thought it would be fun to do a scrapbook based on the old drinking game we played back in college, I Never. Like the game, this type of album would be best shared among close friends, although I suppose it would work as a pretty effective icebreaker as well. It's a good opportunity to journal about some interesting things you may have done in your past, or to speculate about what you'd never ever do and why. Or just make up a whole secret life if you want! It's your album, anything goes!

TIPS AND TECH

This layout began with a digital photo that I altered in Adobe Photoshop. I selected my head and shoulders from one photo and cut and pasted them onto a new image background that I created with several layers of dingbat-font characters and Photoshop brushes. I then added more layers over the top of my image. After printing the photo, I embellished it further with glitter and gems. The title was created in Microsoft Word Art, and the journaling was handwritten. To finish, I inked around the whole page with a black ink pad.

SUPPLIES

Fonts: Animals, Star Time Too JL, Shagadelic Bold; Brushes: Downloaded from Justlia.com.br, Operafloozy.com, Truly-Sarah.com; Ink Pad: Tsukineko; Gems: Westrim Crafts; Flower: Marcel Schurman

Kristin Holly is a 35-year-old ex-librarian and the mother of three young children. What she enjoys most about scrapbooking is challenging herself to create layouts with fresh topics and a unique journaling perspective. "I love to incorporate humor, creative writing, and research into my layouts," she says. "My style is truly mixed-media, as I combine computer-generated elements with techniques such as acrylic and watercolor painting, stamping, sewing, and metal work." Holly's husband of seven years is her favorite travel companion; together they have visited exciting locales such as Bali, Thailand, the Philippines, Australia, and New Zealand, and have even lived on the island of Guam. They currently reside in Katy, Texas.

TRISECTOR

MOTIVATION

I created this scrapbook for my dad's 65th surprise birthday party. It was meant to serve as a guest sign-in book as well as a photo/memory book. The triangular shape made it a great stand-up centerpiece as guests arrived, though that was incidental to my true motivation for its shape.

My father is a philosopher/mathematician. He has written philosophy about the holy trinity and published a book of math theory, *The Trisection of Angles*. With the website name: geocities.com/trisector, it was obvious to me that this was the shape it had to be!

TIPS AND TECH

The materials for this scrapbook were all purchased from Kate's Paperie on Broadway in SoHo, NY. The corrugated paper appealed to me for the cover. It gave the book some strength, and I felt its geometric texture complimented its triangular shape. Also, the printed-wood pattern gave it a masculine feel. The inside papers I alternated, cream and black. The black paper had a groove, which echoed the corrugated texture on the cover. I thought they made a nice backdrop for the mostly black and white photos inside, and the light cream was perfect for journaling. I built it simply, by just having the pages fit into one another on the fold and binding them with a black-and-gold cord. The finishing touch was a black silk ribbon to tie it closed.

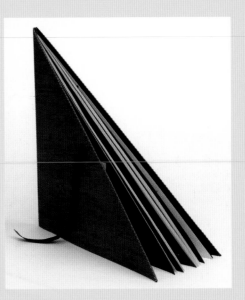

I grew up in Brooklyn, NY and studied in NYC, where I obtained a BFA from Cooper Union. I now live in Staten Island with my husband and daughter and work as a graphic designer for Saatchi and Saatchi Healthcare, NY. I love creating one-of-a-kind custom scrapbooks and have begun a business doing just that. My website is: myenchantedscrapbook.com. It is also a dream of mine to have a children's book I've been working on published in the near future.

BORN TO ONE

While I've known I was adopted for as long as I can remember, I've never known why I was adopted. Many people in my life have always questioned me and my thoughts on the subject. The only answer I can ever give them is...

For whatever reason my birth mother gave me up, she felt she couldn't provide me with what I deserved. I thank this unknown woman for such a selfless act of courage.

For my parents, the only parents I have are the BEST. Sure, we might argue from time to time like any family but the unconditional love is...

dAUGHTER To another

116

BORN TO ONE, DAUGHTER TO ANOTHER

Janene Jaeger

MOTIVATION

As I grow older, my appreciation for my parents grows stronger, as I would imagine any child would admit. Recently a friend of mine had an abortion, and it made me evaluate one's options for an unwanted birth.

Thankfully, I have never had to make such a decision, nor would I want to. My birth mother could have easily made other decisions, but she gave me up for adoption. I was fortunate for that, but also for the parents I do have. Both my sister and I were adopted from separate mothers. Eleven years later, my mother gave birth to my brother. My parents have never treated us different or showed more love for one over another. I think they are the most amazing people.

TIPS AND TECH

To create a little texture to the page, and for lack of rub-ons, I cut an "O" out of cardboard and adhered pattered paper over it to create the "O" in "To."
I used the positioning of the ribbon to slice a pocket for the tag with journaling, so it is easy to pull in and out.

I used Basic Grey monograms for the "D" in Daughter. I had already used that particular letter, so I used the negative portion of the stencil from the background and cut out a "D" with different patterned paper from Basic Grey.

SUPPLIES

Patterned Papers: Paperloft, Foofala, Basic Grey; Cardstock: Bazzill; Rub-Ons: 7gypsies, Foofala; Letter Stickers: Basic Grey, Ink: Ranger; Ribbon: Foofala and unknown.

"I enjoy scrapbooking because I am constantly challenged and striving to please myself," Janene Jaeger says. "I'm almost always wishing my layouts would turn out different or better, and I think that's what makes me want to keep working at it time and again." What started out as a pastime has grown into a passion for Jaeger. In 2005, she and her business partner Dina started ZSIAGE, a scrapbook-paper manufacturing company that strives to fill the voids in the industry by creating galleries not found anywhere else. After moving from New York to Texas to Connecticut and back to New York, Jaeger is currently living single in the city.

2005 Pubster
Panty Journal

Panties to fit my every mood

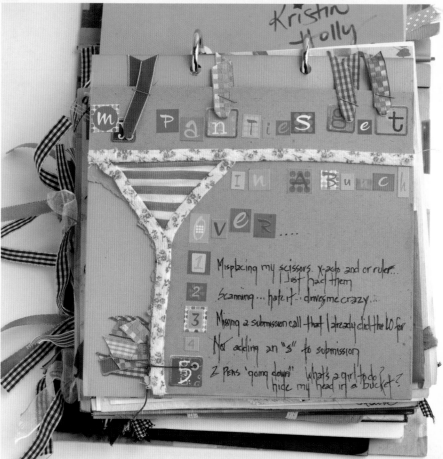

Kristin Holly

M Panties S et

In A Bunch

Ever....

1. Misplacing my scissors, x-acto and or ruler... I just had them

2. Scanning... hate it... drives me crazy...

3. Missing a submission call that I already did the LO for

4. Not adding an "s" to submission

5. 2 Peas "going down" what's a girl to do? I hide my head in a bucket?

Slim Pickin's

How I became a Thong girl

PANTY JOURNAL

MOTIVATION

The thought process behind the "Panty Journal" began innocently enough on a message board. A question was posed to all members as to what panties they wear and if they reflect who they really are. The conversation began in an amusing manner, but as it happens in real life, introspection became more apparent. We openly shared our misgivings, our joys, and the reasons we sported certain undergarments, and before long the idea of a circle journal was presented. The rest as they say is history.

Women from around the globe shared their personal stories of the panty and a book was born.

When in BLOOMERS

I am soft, VULNERablE, and as Sweet As A Flower!

In the past several years, Margert Ann Kruljac's work has started to reflect her personal experiences, thoughts and musings. "I find that through texture and color, I am able to bring to life memories of not only the significant occasions that mark the passing of time, but also those tiny treasured snippets of life that, left unrecorded, would quickly be forgotten," she says. Kruljac's work has been published in *Somerset Studios*, *Legacy*, *Memory Makers*, *Pinecone Press*, *Altered Arts*, and *Ivy Cottage*.

experience

A tender gaze, chin cradled by a strong masculine hand, a supple kiss that grows, music plays in the distance from an orchestra that cannot be seen, the heavens lit with color.

For me the first time was none of the things my mind's eye had pictured, what Hollywood and primetime television had assured me it would be. In my theater, meaningful gazes and lingering touches were replaced with fear, embarrassment and a rapid succession of movements that left me wondering what all the fuss was about.

Now that I'm well into my thirties, I have come to realize that it is a living breathing entity of its own. Ever changing and evolving. Gone are the days of hesitation and uneasiness. With the right person, someone with whom you have built a life, those same emotions are replaced with anticipation and, dare I say, a bit of confidence. As we grow, both in age and understanding, so does one's sex life. You learn to appreciate the stolen brief moments of primal need and yet realize that YES!

May 2005

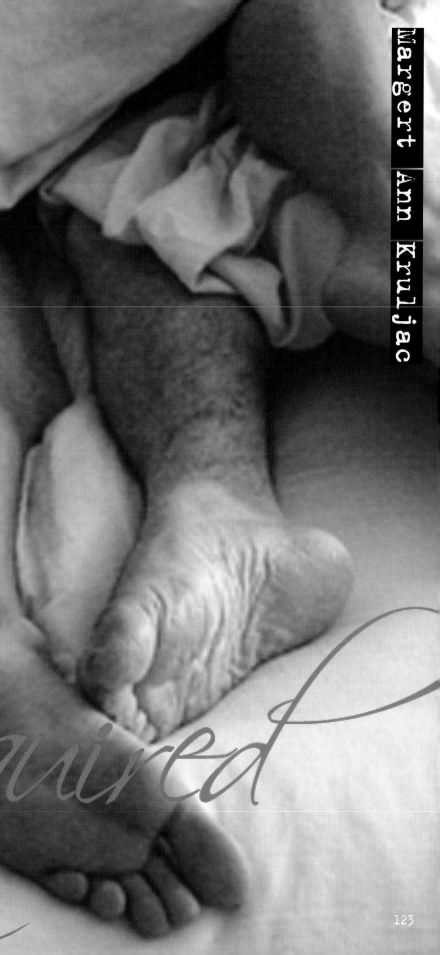

As women, this is what we are taught fom the time
we are very small, that sex, especially that first time, is full of
romance, pomp and circumstance, fireworks and fantasy...
Yet, reality is often very, very different.

Sex, it would seem, is like anything else in life.
Given the right circumstances, the right person and, yes,
experience, it has the amazing ability to become all
of the things that you had envisioned it would be.

There actually is an orchestra...
Only now you know that you
are the one playing the mesmerizing tune.

35 years of age

Required

TWENTY YEARS FROM NOW
YOU WILL BE MORE DISAPPOINTED
BY THE THINGS YOU DIDN'T DO
THAN BY THE ONES YOU DID.
SO THROW OFF THE BOWLINES.
SAIL AWAY FROM THE SAFE HARBOR.
CATCH THE TRADE WINDS IN YOUR SAILS.

EXPLORE. DREAM.
DISCOVER.

(UNKNOWN)

MOVING TO PHILADELPHIA

Elizabeth Thorpe

MOTIVATION

I was given a new scrapbook as a going-away present. The idea was to document my experiences in Philadelphia to share with my friends in Maine. I did some of the early pages right away, but then I got stuck. I couldn't get excited about listing all the things I did in chronological order, so I decided to create pages that showed different things I love about the city. Because I love all the old buildings, I took pictures of some of them and made them into a collage. I plan to do the same with parks, museums, etc. The greeting card on the first page was one that I had on the wall in my cubicle when I was still living in Maine. I love Maine, so it was very hard for me to leave. This quote helped motivate me to overcome my inertia and explore new places.

TIPS AND TECH

The first page is the inside front cover of my "Moving To Philadelphia" album. I had some leftover address labels, so I used those to cover the page. I stuck the greeting card on with clear photo corners. When I finish my album, I'm planning to write a table of contents inside the card.

SUPPLIES

Tinfoil, Ranger Pigment Ink Pad, Stampcraft letter stamps (Typewriter), EK Success Star punch, Greeting card, Address labels.

Elizabeth Thorpe is a writer from Maine who now lives in Philadelphia. She has a degree in English from the University of Maine and an MFA in writing from Goddard College. Besides reading and writing, she enjoys photography, traveling, and going to concerts. She is currently working on a final revision of her first novel, *Lydia's Island*, among other writing projects.

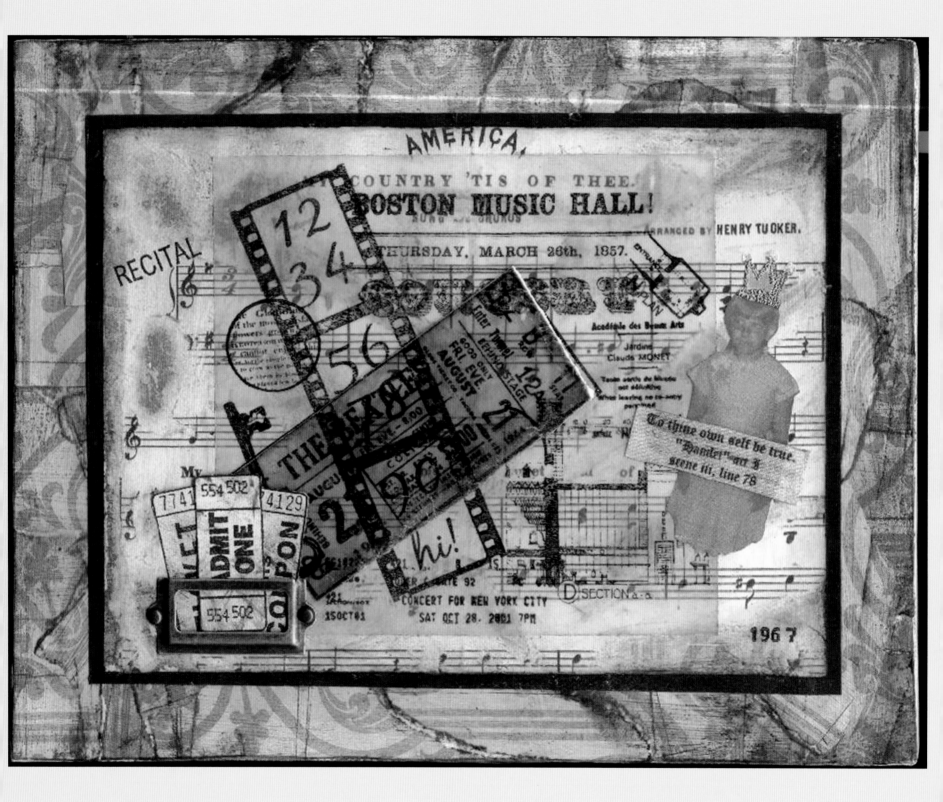

RECITAL

MOTIVATION

My motivation was twofold.
1.) I wanted to highlight a series of stamps that I had contributed to the design of. 2.) I enjoy working on canvas and this was a memory I had yet to document. It would be one of those creations that I would hoped observers would ponder over—attempting to discover the story hidden within.

TIPS AND TECH

The focal point of the collage was created by stamping images onto vellum. I had sketched and stamped the pattern to practice before transferring the arrangement to the vellum. The mat for the vellum was created with the peeled-paper technique.

The music-patterned paper was adhered to another patterned paper. Strips of masking tape were applied to the top sheet of paper and then peeled off, tearing the paper along with it, exposing the underneath patterned paper layer. The vellum was adhered to this mat, and then the additional stamping of Recital and 1967 were added. A copper bookplate was secured with brads to the lower left-hand corner to house hand-stamped tickets. A photo of myself at my first piano recital was added, along with a quote from Hamlet. A gold crown was stamped, embossed, and adhered to the picture. Mica was cut to highlight the ticket, which was stamped in the college on vellum, and to draw the eye across the canvas from the tickets to the crown. The edges were inked prior to mounting onto black cardstock.

The canvas was created to frame the matted collage. Pieces of paper were torn and inked prior to being adhered to the canvas with a matte gel medium. The matted collage was then placed on the canvas with additional coats of matte gel medium.

SUPPLIES

Leave Memories: rubber stamps, proverbial, bookplate. Ranger Nick Bantok and Tim Holtz: inks; embossing powder/ink, stickles. StazOn: ink. USArtQuest: mica. Paperbilities and Basic Grey: patterned papers. Papers and More, Marcos Paper: cardstock. Fredrix: canvas. Vellum.

A wife and mother residing in the Metro Detroit area, Jill Jones-Lazuka displays her love of family not only in real time, but also through the research and compilation of her family's history. Her interest in mixed media surfaced shortly before she decided to take a break from the music ministry in which she was involved, and over the last few years she has begun to focus on combining that interest with memory preservation. Her articles, tips, and creations have appeared in *The Book Artist Zine*, *Stamp & Scrap Arts*, *Growing Up Me*, and *The Book of Us*, as well as on various online scrapbooking sites. Jones-Lazuka is available for freelance design, teaching, and writing assignments for the memory arts-community. She can be reached at serendipity@christinagirl.com.

10 REASONS to STAY SINGLE

- No In-Laws
- No need to change your name
- You can hog the covers and sleep in the middle of the bed
- You can be inconsiderate and eat all the ice cream
- No one argues with you about how to squeeze the toothpaste
- There's never a line for the bathroom
- You don't have to explain why you own 20 pairs of black shoes
- No one tells you not to spend your last $15 on a manicure
- You can pick up and travel on a moments notice
- You always get to choose the movie

April 2005

10 REASONS TO STAY SINGLE

Robin Cecil

MOTIVATION

No In-Laws; no need to change to change your last name; you can hog the covers and sleep in the middle of the bed; you can be inconsiderate and eat all the ice cream; no one argues with you about how to squeeze the toothpaste; there's never a line for the bathroom; you don't have to explain why you own 20 pairs of black shoes; no one tells you not to spend your last $15 on a manicure; you can pick up and travel on a moment's notice; you always get to choose the movie. April 2005.

SUPPLIES

Fonts: Autumn Leaves (AL) Highlight. AL Professor downloaded from peasinabucket.com and Barbara Hand.
Avatar created by Dawn Stocstill from a personal photo (www.hunibuniscreations.com or download mix-and-match chicks by Dawn Stocstill, available at www.scrapbook-bytes.com/store).
Polaroid from Holly McCaig's "New Beginnings" kit, available at www.thedigichick.com.
Background papers and elements from Holly McCaig's "Winter Wonder" kit available at www.thedigichick.com.

Robin Cecil was introduced to scrapbooking back in 2000, when it could take days to create one layout. With her background in information technology, making the switch from paper to digital was a "no-brainer," and she can now complete layouts in fifteen minutes. Although Cecil never thought of herself as the crafty type, she has become passionate about digital scrapbooking, which allows her to use technology to document important family values, traditions, advice, and life lessons to pass on to her son. Cecil's work has been published in *Simple Scrapbooks*, *Creating Keepsakes*, and *Memory Makers*. She is a member of the creative team for www.thedigichick.com and has just launched her own digital scrapbooking site, www.digitalscrapbookdesigns.com.

EMILY'S

CLASSICAL

AMERICAN

OUR HOME IS A JUMBLE OF MEXICAN ART AND ANTIQUES. MATT AND I LOVE OUR BRIGHTLY COLORED WALLS AND QUIRKY COLLECTIBLES. TOGETHER WE'VE TRANSFORMED OUR 50'S CLASSIC HOUSE INTO A FUNKY AND FUN RETREAT WHERE WE CAN JUST RELAX AND LAUGH TOGETHER.

CHAOS

THE MAGIC SCRAPS DESIGN TEAM
EMILY'S WORLD—ECLECTIC BOHEMIAN

MOTIVATION

Ashley, Kate, and I are the creative team behind the scrapbook company Magic Scraps.

Balancing our friendship, work relationship, and stress while collaborating on artistic designs are only a few of the challenges we face every day. With these layouts, we wanted to give you a glimpse of each of our senses of style and what inspires us individually. We celebrate our similarities as well as our individuality as women and artists with fresh, unique looks, which hopefully will inspire women to showcase their sense of personal style.

TIPS AND TECH

Don't be afraid to use patterned papers or elements in your layouts. Balance out heavy patterns with subtle tinted transparencies.

SUPPLIES

Background Paper: Basic Grey. Patterned Papers (including title blocks): Design Originals. Red and Clear Transparencies, Clear Colors: Magic Scraps. Black Label Holder and All Mini Fasteners: Magic Scraps. Photo Anchors: Junkitz. Colored 2-Fold Fasteners: Magic Scraps. Rub-On Letters: Lil' Davis. Font: Garbageschrift Thin.

Emily Adams is the education coordinator for Magic Scraps. Her job covers creating samples, writing everything from classes to packaging instructions, and figuring out creative new uses for products. She and her husband, Matt, have been married for six years. Adams is the artsy-grungy type; her contrast of style and blunt opinions gives Magic Scraps' design collaborations a liberal balance (and occasionally a little drama).

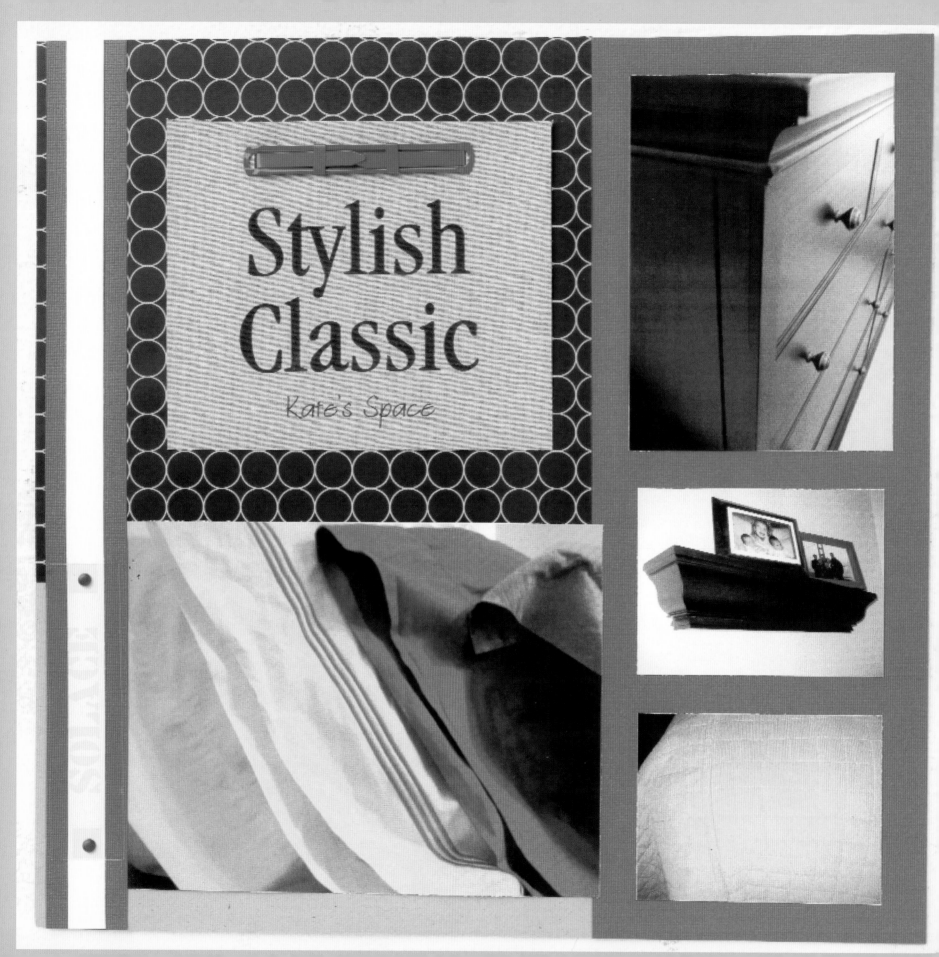

Stylish Classic

Kate's Space

THE MAGIC SCRAPS DESIGN TEAM

STYLISH CLASSIC—KATE'S SPACE

TIPS AND TECH

Add extra texture by incorporating fabrics into your layouts. Some scrapbooking fabrics are even printable, so the possibilities are almost limitless!

SUPPLIES
All Cardstock: Bazzill Basics Paper. Patterned Paper: Magic Scraps. Transparency Clear Details: Magic Scraps. Mini Fasteners: Magic Scraps. Fabric Paper: Magic Scraps. Colored 2-Fold Fastener: Magic Scraps.

As associate creative director for Magic Scraps, Kate Lynch does everything from laying out ads to creating graphic designs for new products. She is the office "finisher," a dedicated worker with a free spirit. A graduate of Texas A&M University, she is also a proud Aggie. Her style is conservative and classic, and her attention to detail is always evident in her designs.

Suburban Retro
Life at 1200

After 12 years of marriage, Ben and I finally became the proud owners of a 4 bedroom, 2.5 bath home built in 1973. While it wasn't exactly our dream home, we both had vision and determiniation to transform it into a special place for our family. Now, this is the only house I ever want.

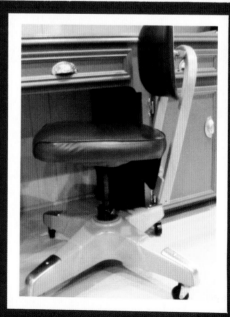

Our home in Richardson, TX

THE MAGIC SCRAPS DESIGN TEAM
SUBURBAN RETRO—LIFE AT 1200

Kitchen
Color: Holiday Turquoise

Living Room
Color: Mandarin

Den Trim
Color: Superior Bronze

Den Walls
Color: Universal Khaki

PlayRoom
Color: Hep Green

Entry Hall
Color: Stirring Orange

Nolen's Room
Color: Reflecting Pool

My Love for decorating was a gift from my mother. She made me spend countless hours flipping through decorating magazines, pretending like I really cared whether or not we should paint the kitchen Gypsy Red or Cherry Tomato. As a child, it all looked the same. But as an adult, I realized the beauty of color and what a difference it could make. Why my mother had paintchips tacked all over the house now makes sense. I have lots of influences that come together to create a unique style that is all my own. Besides my mother, I'm influenced by the 50s and 60's, disco, jazz, Vegas, my kids, vintage office supplies, the Far East and the Texas coast.

TIPS AND TECHS
Create a color palette for your home using a blank film-strip overlay. Print names of rooms and paint colors on coordinating cardstock, cut down, and use under trans-parency to create a unique page border.

SUPPLIES
All Cardstock: Bazzill Basics Paper. Virtual Metal: Magic Scraps. Blank Filmstrip Overlay Freeze-Frames: Magic Scraps. Silver Label Holder and Mini Fasteners: Magic Scraps. Fonts: Gill Sans Condensed and Rage Italic.

Ashley Smith began Magic Scraps in 2001, as an effort to keep her scrapbook stores on the cutting edge. Since its whole-sale debut in 2002, Magic Scraps has evolved into a major innovator within the industry, with unique products and aggres-sive educational programs. Smith and her husband, Ben, have been married for fifteen years and have three children. They live in the suburbs of Dallas, Texas, where their house is filled with contemporary retro touches that influence Smith's design tastes.

PAPERBACK *Burlesque!*
by Jo Boobs

Miss Exotic World Of The Great Tassel Twirl Off
STAFF
Miss Exotic World Staff

She Made Passion Pay Off

... in here too!

Saints and Sinners Unite

Burlesque For Beginners:
a burlesque workshop from professor Jo 'Boobs' Weldon

PAPERBACK BURLESQUE

MOTIVATION

My piece is kind of an homage to all the wild women out there. It's also reflective of my historical interest in burlesque and other forms of adult entertainment. It's an affinity that has always been with me and seems like it always will.

Jo Weldon is such a stripper! She got her first taste of live ecdysiasm in 1978, when she peeled off a vintage gown at a local showing of *The Rocky Horror Picture Show*. When she turned eighteen a few years later, she was legal and ready to hit the strip-joint stage—which she did throughout the early 1980s, to pay her way through college. In addition to producing the annual "Follies Fromage" at Coney Island's Burlesque at the Beach, Weldon currently runs the Bowery School of Burlesque in New York City. She is also a First-Amendment activist, defending the art of stripping as a form of expression, and a labor activist fighting for adult entertainers' rights to compensation and health benefits.

BROTHERS

Journey

The JOURNEY of sharing both laughter and tears, connected TOGETHER through a LIFETIME of years.

BROTHERS' JOURNEY

MOTIVATION

This was only supposed to be a stop along the way to the Grand Canyon. Who would have guessed a mere pit stop to Great Sand Dunes would turn out to be one of the highlights of our summer vacation?

TECHNIQUE

Create background with various shades of Basic Grey papers and Bazzill to outline. All the paper, cardstock, photos, and vellum were distressed with ink. Some pieces were also heat embossed for extra emphasis.

The "BROTHERS" title was created using a stencil alphabet sticker set. I backed it with Basic Grey cardstock and inserted an eyelet into the top of each letter. Then I curled Artistic Wire using a pencil and wove it through the eyelets.

For the subtitles, I stamped and embossed the word Journey. I handwrote Great Sand Dunes Colorado with an embossing pen and heat embossed it. I finished these subtitles with a sticker and metal stencil letter at the beginning of the words. The journaling for the tag under the top right photo was created by printing onto cardstock. Then I ran it through a Xyron sticker machine, and trimmed the words to fit the tag.

The library pocket was created to house more favorite photos. I simply trimmed a photo to fit the front to call attention to it. I also curved the top edge of the library pocket, using a circle cutter, to better see the photos inside.

I adorned the titles, photos, and tags with fibers, brads, and photo corners.

SUPPLIES

Basic Grey Motifica Collection Patterned Papers and Tags. Bazzill Cardstock. EK Success Adornments Fibers. Making Memories Brads. Making Memories Metal Stencil Letter. Life's Journey Metal Frames. Paperbilities Vellum Clocks. Xyron black photo corners. Imprintz Pigment Ink—Black and Copper. M'Bellishments Eyelets. Stampabilities Metallic Embossing Powders. Tim Holz Distress Ink—Vintage Photo. Life's Journey metal words: Remember and Journey. Stencil stickers from Wal-Mart (mfg unknown). Artistic Wire. Copper Color Alphabet Stamps. Library Pocket template downloaded from KindredCreations.com. Creative Memories Circle Cutter. Hootie and Ancient Script Fonts downloaded from ScrapVillage.com. aced metal frames and words on some photos to emphasize them and to keep the eyes moving across the page.

Leisa Tobler is a stay-at-home mother of three who enjoys storytelling at local schools and libraries, volunteering in the community, traveling the country and the globe, and—of course—scrapbooking. Although she began the hobby when her oldest son was a baby as a way to just get photos into a book to share, scrapbooking has grown into a creative passion over the last year. "I use a variety of techniques and materials to evoke the feelings of the event and, hopefully, delight the senses," she says. "As a storyteller, I see scrapbooking as a way to transport us back to the moment in time where our memories were created."

Images of France

GORDES SUR CIEL - APTLY NAMED WHEN YOU SEE IT RISING DRAMATICALLY ABOVE THE EARLY MORNING MIST, SEEMINGLY AFLOAT IN THE SKY. ONE OF THE BEST PRESERVED MEDIAEVAL VILLAGES I HAVE EVER SEEN, THE HOUSES CLING TO STEEP TWISTY STREETS OF DUSTY OCHRE. CENTURIES OF TRAFFIC AND HORSES HAVE LEFT THEIR MARK IN THE DEEP WARPED GROOVES IN THE COBBLED ROADS.

WE WALKED THE WHOLE WAY TO THE TOP AND WERE REWARDED WITH A PANORAMIC VIEW OF THE SURROUNDING REGION. THE VILLAGE IS PEPPERED WITH "ATELIERS" RANGING FROM JEWELLERS TO PRINTMAKERS TO BASKET WEAVERS. THE JEWEL FOR ME WAS THE STUDIO OF A BOOKBINDER AND CALLIGRAPHER WHERE WE FOUND THE MOST BEAUTIFUL BINDINGS IN EMBOSSED AND TOOLED LEATHER.

Archways intrigue me..

IMAGES OF FRANCE

MOTIVATION

In this spread I created my own handpainted backgrounds, inspired by the colors of southern France, where we often have holidays. The earth is a rich red ochre with dense vivid green forests and milky turquoise lakes. Colors like that scream out to be captured!

I also like to use colors and techniques which give a weathered, aged or tarnished look to the pages. For example, I like the crinkles that you get with too much glue, or a slightly dog-eared corner. I like it when the book won't close properly; you must entice it and dig in to find out what interesting things are stuck to the pages.

TIPS AND TECH

Background Technique
The backgrounds are created on colored cardstock (one yellow, one peach) using Stewart Gill paints. The paint has been applied using a palette knife in much the same way as buttering a slice of bread. These paints have a beautiful translucent quality, which means I can layer colors until I am happy with the results. I have also used a coarse bristle brush to create definite brush marks in places, or a sponge where I wanted the colors softer. As well as matte colors, I have used Alchemy paints, which are shot through with a secondary color, causing the paint to react differently depending on the underlying color. On the first page, I have made extensive use of the Clearsnap stylus tool to create repeated pattern. This tool has a range of different shaped tips, white tips are made from soft sponge and can be used to apply color, black tips are firmer and when gently heated will take an impression from a textured surface. Here I have used a square tip pressed onto a butterfly rubber stamp for my pattern. To apply the color, I have applied the paints to Cut 'n Dry foam, then picked up the color with the stylus tool and applied various colors in patches around the page.

Glenda Waterworth is not an avid scrapbooker, fastidiously recording every event of any significance. She prefers using her pages to capture the atmosphere and mood she felt when she took a photograph. "I am not particularly interested in creating an heirloom for a future generation," she admits. "I'm creating something that gives me pleasure by reminding me of the good times." Waterworth was born in northern England and currently lives in Teesdale, a land of wide-open spaces and windswept, heather-clad moorland. She runs a rubber-stamping company and paper-craft mail-order business with her husband, Adrian, and is "mum" to two fascinating cats, Basil and Sesame.

ALBI IS THE NEAREST LARGE TOWN AND IS FULL OF INTERESTING MEDIAEVAL ARCHITECTURE. WE WALKED AROUND SOME OF THE OLD STREETS WHERE WOAD MERCHANTS BUILT FINE HOUSES TO SHOW OFF THEIR WEALTH.

Colours excite me ...

THIS ONE INCLUDED CARVINGS OF THE FAMILY, SITUATED IN A CHARMING SECLUDED COURTYARD. SHOWING OFF WEALTH, YET KEEPING THE TREASURES HIDDEN IN A VERY PRIVATE SPACE. WAS THIS A TROPHY WIFE OR A PROTECTED DAUGHTER?

On the second page, I have created a slightly different look by using the edge of my palette knife to scratch into the wet paint.

Images

All my images were created using a digital camera, so I was able to use Photoshop to crop them all to a standard size. They were printed onto a glossy photopaper using quality printing, and then layered onto slightly larger black paper to give a thin frame.

Journaling Text

The text was typed using a shareware font, Sterofidelic, with headings in P22 Cézanne. All the text was printed onto inkjet acetate so that the colors could shine through. I chose to print my text reversed so that the ink side is actually next to the paper, this helps to prevent the ink from scratching off the acetate as the pages are handled.

Adhesives and Fixings

I used a Xyron machine to apply adhesive to the photographs and mats. The acetate was applied using Dimensional Magic, an embellishment adhesive and glaze that dries to a hard glossy finish. Only a couple of spots are needed, though in places I have deliberately coated the whole piece of acetate and let the glaze seep out around the edges.

The tag was applied with a double-sided foam pad. One piece of acetate was applied to the page, using tiny pewter brads rather than adhesives.

Tag Photoshop Tutorial

The tag on this page was created using Photoshop version 7.0.

1. Start with a high resolution photo (a minimum 300 dpi) with good contrast. From the IMAGE menu, select MODE and change your image to GREYSCALE.
2. Try adjusting the contrast and brightness by selecting the IMAGE menu, then ADJUSTMENTS then BRIGHTNESS/CONTRAST.
3. Convert your grayscale image to pure black and white. From the IMAGE menu, select ADJUSTMENTS, then POSTERIZE. This will ask for a value, if you select 2, then Photoshop will adjust your photograph to use the two values of pure black and pure white. If you choose 3, you will also have a mid tone of gray included. Choose a higher value and Photoshop will include more shades of gray accordingly, so you can play with your image until you see a result you like.
4. Save your image!
5. From your tools palette, select the magic wand tool and click somewhere on your photograph that is white.

This should highlight a selection with a dashed line. If only a single white area has been selected, choose the SELECT menu and click on SIMILAR and this should then highlight all white areas in your image.
6. From the SELECT menu, click INVERSE. (You could just click on a black area, but this catches any shades of gray if you have used the posterize command)
7. Once all non-white areas have been selected, click the EDIT menu and click COPY.
8. Open your background image and click EDIT, then PASTE.
9. Your black and white image should now be layered on top of your colored background. Select the move tool from the tools palette and you can move your image around until it is sitting where you want it.
10. Once you are happy, save your new image and print out on best quality. Use an existing tag as a template and cut your image into a tag shape. Punch a hole and thread with decorative fibers.

UNTITLED

MOTIVATION

My scrapbook pages are excerpts from a visual journal exploring femininity, body image, and womanhood. I enjoyed using vintage images as well as modern materials, as the quest to find a balanced self-image as a woman is universal and timeless.

TIPS AND TECH

I have a large collection of scrapbooking materials, which is vital in my creative process. I keep a huge, evolving box of various papers, which includes colorful and transparent plastics, origami paper, junk mail, texts in foreign languages, postcards, scraps of watercolor paintings and drawings, ripped-out pages of old art books, stamps, color Xeroxes of interesting items, letters, decorative napkins, old paper dolls and their clothing, images from magazines, old maps, ticket stubs, wallpaper samples, doodles, vintage photos, and handmade papers. It is essentially a big collection of scraps. Having an abundance of interesting supplies to choose from and play with allows for the art piece to evolve and grow in surprising ways.

My other essentials when scrapbooking include glue sticks, scissors, a variety of drawing supplies, and a big table where I can lay out various ideas side by side and make a big mess. I also sometimes sew images to the paper, so I keep out a sewing kit with various colors of thread and yarn. I pull out my calligraphy set and a tiny set of alphabet stamps as well, which are great for adding text. I like to have all of my supplies visible and readily available.

In these scrapbook pages I made several handmade envelopes out of various papers found in my collection box. The first envelope is made from plastic, which was used to wrap a bouquet of flowers; I liked the lacy, see-through quality. I use a variety of envelope templates to design my envelopes; the templates come in an assortment of sizes and shapes.

I love using envelopes. They can be filled with a couple of snapshots, a line of poetry, a little drawing, or a memento. I like the layering and the surprise and secrecy that they afford. Along this same vein, I often layer with see-through materials as well. As you can see on the first page, a piece of acetate is layered over the words "hold fast."
It is easy to add these additional small flipping pages inside larger pages of a scrapbook. Simply fold the paper you would like to add, making a strip. With the glue stick, adhere the strip to your page. Like the envelopes, this gives you a structure on your page that can be opened and closed.

SUPPLIES

Envelope templates from Judi Kins. www.judikins.com

I also highly recommend the small alphabet and letter stamps, "Stamp Squares" from all night media rubber stamps. They have a large assortment of their alphabet/letter sets, which can be found at www.plaidonline.com. (I did not use them on any of the submitted pages, but they are wonderful and I use them frequently.)

I'm Not You

With one master's degree in art therapy from Pratt Institute and another in social work from Columbia University, Sarah Vollmann keeps busy dividing her time between her studio and her work as an art therapist/social worker. She has shown her art in galleries and exhibits in New York City and throughout the country, and although she works primarily as a painter in oil and encaustic, she also enjoys printmaking, collage, and creating scrapbooks. Vollmann also works as a teaching artist for the Museum for African Art in New York City. She lives in the area with her husband, Barry, and dog, Zora.

HOOPS WORD SEARCH
Search the jumbled letters for...

E X E B O R S O E O H O
T F T C A C T I V I T Y
D A E R Y Y R Y X W H H
H E X E R C I S E H I
A F U I M A P A
F U N E T L E V

WRIGLEY'S SPEARMINT
NOW LONGER LASTING

START ▶

MAZE DAZE

FINISH ✗

MACADAM CROSSWORD
Use the clues below to help solve the playground puzzler.

1. Earn your --------
2. Born to ---
3. People you know and trust
4. Let's ---- a game
5. Physical games

How To Get More

146

HOW TO GET MORE AND MYRTLE BEACH MAP

Bonnie Jean Woolger

MOTIVATION

Inspiration for the layout: What motivates me to do these books? I am motivated by my desires:

• To document and treasure the ordinary: everyday objects, experiences, and events.

• To maintain my sanity in a world that seems to be out-of-control.

• To create my art in an environment where time is compressed.

• To make my art portable and accessible.

BONNIE'S RECIPE FOR A SCRAPBOOK PAGE:

Begin with blank book (home-made or store-bought). Add some found objects: Photos, Wrappers, Labels, Junk mail, Magazine clip-pings, or any other scrap of paper that can be glued down.

Using Elmer's school glue or a glue stick (consider some-thing archival)stick those bits of paper to the blank page.

Now, with a mark-making tool-Pencil, Pen, Colored pencil, Gel or other colored pen, Spiro graph, Blo-pen, Crayon, Marker, Watercolor paint (simple children's kits), Acrylic paint-record the events and feelings among the words and images you have glued down. Then repeat the process until the book is full. Enjoy the journey.

ADDITIONAL INGREDIENTS:
Rulers, Templates, Stencils,
A variety of papers,
Children's "art kits,"
Punches, Stamps, Stickers,
Doodads people give you.
Myrtle Beach map

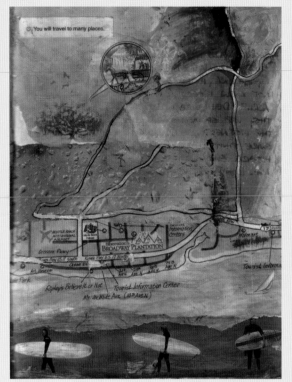

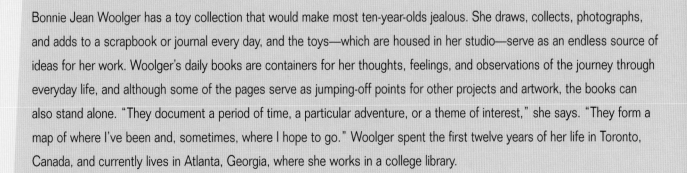

Bonnie Jean Woolger has a toy collection that would make most ten-year-olds jealous. She draws, collects, photographs, and adds to a scrapbook or journal every day, and the toys—which are housed in her studio—serve as an endless source of ideas for her work. Woolger's daily books are containers for her thoughts, feelings, and observations of the journey through everyday life, and although some of the pages serve as jumping-off points for other projects and artwork, the books can also stand alone. "They document a period of time, a particular adventure, or a theme of interest," she says. "They form a map of where I've been and, sometimes, where I hope to go." Woolger spent the first twelve years of her life in Toronto, Canada, and currently lives in Atlanta, Georgia, where she works in a college library.

Applicant's Name __Deborah__

Applicant's Address _____

III. Supervisory Activities (It will be especially helpful to us, should the applicant be judged to need further supervised experience, to know specifically which supervisory activities were used and how often)
   A. Together worked with clients

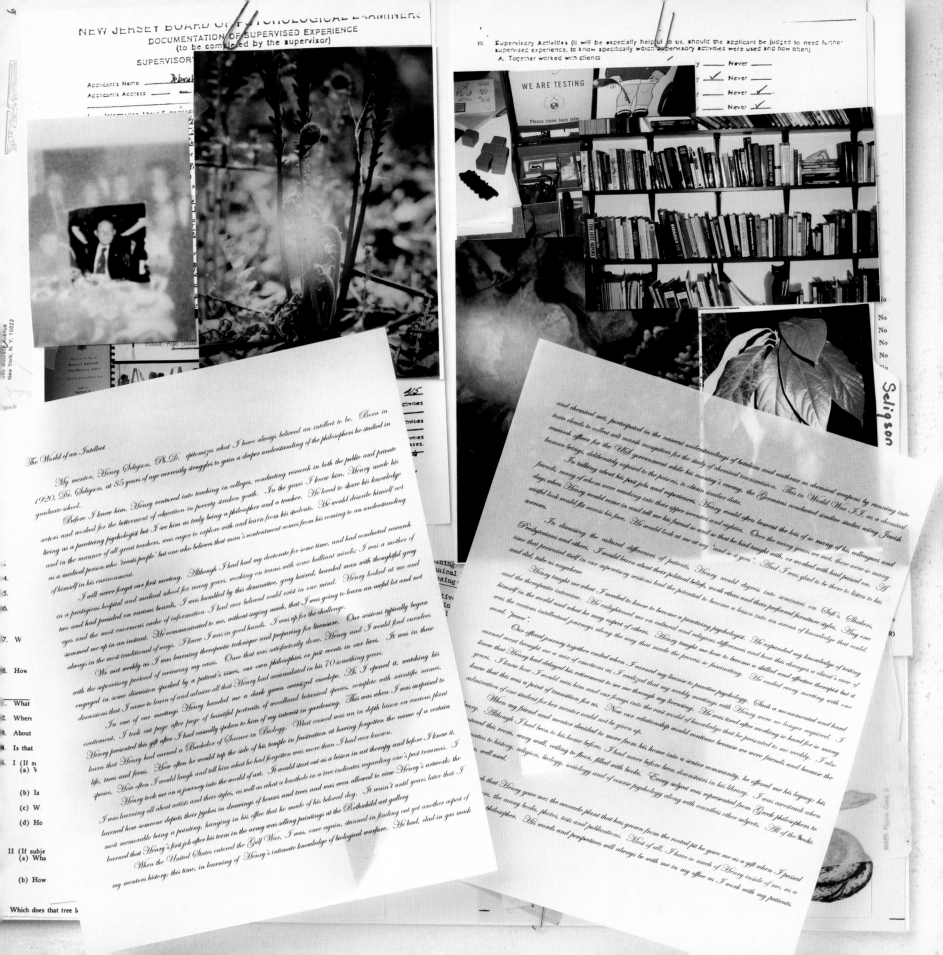

WE ARE TESTING
Please come back later

590 Madison Avenue
New York, N.Y. 10022

Seligson

No
No
No
No

The World of an Intellect

My mentor, Henry Seligson, Ph.D., epitomizes what I have always believed an intellect to be. Born in 1920, Dr. Seligson, at 85 years of age currently struggles, to gain a deeper understanding of the philosophers he studied in graduate school.

Before I knew him, Henry ventured into teaching in colleges, conducting research in both the public and private sectors and worked for the betterment of education in poverty stricken youth. In the years, I knew him, Henry made his living as a practicing psychologist but I see him as truly being a philosopher and a teacher. He would describe himself not and in the manner of all great teachers, was eager to explore with and learn from his students. He would come to an understanding as a medical person who 'treats people' but one who believes that man's contentment comes from his coming to an understanding of himself in his environment.

I will never forget our first meeting. Although I had had my doctorate for some time, and had conducted research in a prestigious hospital and medical school for many years, working on teams with some brilliant minds; I was a mother of two and had presided on various boards. I was humbled by this diminutive, gray haired, bearded man with thoughtful gray eyes and the most enormous cache of information I had ever believed could exist in one mind. Henry looked at me and summed me up in an instant. He communicated to me, without saying much, that I was going to learn an awful lot and not always in the most traditional of ways. I knew I was in good hands. I was up for the challenge.

We met weekly as I was learning therapeutic technique and preparing for licensure. Our sessions typically began with the supervisory protocol of reviewing my cases. Once that was satisfactorily done, Henry and I would find ourselves engaged in some discussion sparked by a patient's issues, our own philosophies or just events in our lives. It was in those discussions that I came to learn of and admire all that Henry had accumulated in his 70 something years.

In one of our meetings, Henry handed me a dark green oversized envelope. As I opened it, watching his excitement, I took out page after page of beautiful portraits of woodland botanical species, complete with scientific names. This was when I was surprised to learn that Henry had earned a Bachelor of Science in Biology. What ensued was an in depth lesson on various plant life, trees and ferns. How often he would tap the side of his temple in frustration at having forgotten the name of a certain species. How often I would laugh and tell him what he had forgotten was more than I had ever known.

Henry presented this gift after I had casually spoken to him of my interest in gardening. This was when I was surprised to learn all about artists and their styles, as well as what a knothole in a tree indicates regarding one's past traumas. I learned how someone depicts their psyches in drawings of houses and trees and was even allowed to view Henry's artwork: the most memorable being a painting, hanging in his office that he made of his beloved dog. It wasn't until years later that I learned that Henry's first job after his term in the army was selling paintings at the Rothschild art gallery.

When the United States entered the Gulf War, I was, once again, stunned in finding out yet another aspect of my mentor's history; this time, in learning of Henry's intimate knowledge of biological warfare. He had, clad in gas mask

and chemical suit, participated in the nascent understandings of botulism and anthrax as chemical weapons by running into toxic clouds to collect salt marsh mosquitoes for the study of chemical transmission. This in World War II, as a chemical research officer for the US government while his country's enemy, the Germans conducted similar studies using Jewish human beings, deliberately exposed to the patients, to obtain similar data.

In talking about his past jobs and experiences, Henry would often lament the loss of so many of his friends, many of whom were reaching into their upper seventies and eighties, days when Henry would come in and tell me his friend so and so that he had taught with, or worked with had passed on. A wistful look would flit across his face. He would look at me at say "and so it goes". And I was glad to be there to listen to his sorrows.

In discussing the cultural differences of patients, Henry would digress into seminars on Sufi's, Shakers, Presbyterians and others. I would learn about their political beliefs, work ethics and their preferred furniture styles. Any one time that presented itself in our supervisory sessions had the potential to become a lesson into an arena of knowledge that could and did, take us anywhere.

Henry taught me what I needed to know to become a practicing psychologist. He expanded my knowledge of testing and the therapeutic interview. He enlightened me on cultural and religious differences and how this changes a client's view of himself in the world and what he may expect of others. Henry taught me how to become a skilled and effective therapist but it was the various intellectual journeys along the way that made the process so fascinating.

Over official journey together ended when I earned my license to practice psychology. He ended every meeting with one world, 'peace'. Such a monumental meeting with Henry were no longer required. I knew how I would miss him and our forays into the vast world of knowledge that he presented to me weekly. I earned event brought me a mix of emotions as I realized that my weekly meetings with Henry were no longer required. I knew that Henry had delayed his retirement to see me through my weekly meetings but it years. I knew how I would miss him and our forays into the vast world of knowledge that he presented to me weekly. I knew that this was a point of transition for us. Now our relationship would continue that he presented to me weekly. admiration of one student for her mentor could not be given up. Such a monumental meeting with Henry were no longer required.

When my friend and mentor decided to move from his home into a senior community, he offered me his legacy: his ____ary. Although I had been to his home before, I had never before been downstairs in his library. I was awestruck when ____tered this room, every wall, ceiling to floor, filled with books. Every subject was represented from Greek philosophers to ____uates to history, religion, biology, sociology and of course psychology along with countless other subjects. All of the books ____ well used.

____ch that Henry gave me: the avocado plant that has grown from the rooted pit he gave me as a gift when I passed ____m, the many books, photos, tests and publications. Most of all, I have so much of Henry inside of me, as a ____philosopher. His words and perspectives will always be with me in my office as I work with my patients.

Which does that tree l...

THE WORLD OF AN INTELLECT

MOTIVATION

My scrapbook pages reflect a journey of learning and growth while I was a student under the tutelage of my clinical supervisor, Henry Seligson, PhD. Dr. Seligson and I were introduced after I had made a decision to move from the research and academic world of psychology to the clinical. Henry agreed to supervise me through this multiple-year endeavor. Henry taught me so much more than one in my position expects to learn. I was his student in the broadest sense, learning all I would need to practice in a clinical setting, but so much more. Henry taught me about the world he had lived in and learned from in his seventy-plus years. He was more than a mentor. He became a friend and an inspiration. My depiction of our journey gives me an opportunity to honor all that Henry has taught me and given me. In assembling the collage, I relived and reflected on the time we shared in addition to the lessons I learned. I was his last student before his retirement and hope that what I share in these pages does justice to the gift of this wonderful, brilliant, and inspiring man.

Deborah Wagner is a licensed psychologist running a full-time private practice in Ridgewood, New Jersey. Having earned her master's and doctorate degrees in developmental psychology from the Ferkauf Graduate School of Psychology at Yeshiva University, she now draws on her educational and research background to treat adults, children, and families. Wagner finds her work extremely rewarding and hopes to continue illuminating the path to healing. Her other passion is her family: her son, daughter, husband, and cats. She spends her free time gardening, pursuing artistic endeavors, volunteering in the community, and always seeking more knowledge.

), n. youth [pl. YOUTHS (i
geoguthe < *jugunthi <
*dugunthi- (dr goh, the
base as in YOUNG form
vvencus, ...

DUDE, WHERE'S MY POOL?

CHAMPAGNE
dREaMs
&
CAVIaR
wishES

IT WAS QUIET OUT THERE
MAYBE A LITTLE TOO QUIET...

I OPENED THE DOOR TO THE BACKYARD

AND THERE WAS – MY HUSBAND ♥♥♥

SILENTLY SOAKING UP A FEW REMAINING HOURS OF FREEDOM [BEFORE THE START OF ANOTHER WORK WEEK]

SURROUNDED BY A COUPLE OF TIKKI TORCHES

→ AND A CITRONELLA CANDLE

SCRUNCHED UP IN A TURTLE-SHAPED KIDDIE POOL HE HAD PULLED OUT OF A DUMPSTER.

MAN... YOU COULD NOT GET MORE PATHETIC IF YOU TRIED.

...SCOOCH OVER

DUDE, WHERE'S MY POOL?

Leah Blanco Williams

MOTIVATION

To document life with my husband, Thomas.

TIPS AND TECH

Journaling

It was quiet out there, maybe a little too quiet. I opened the door to the backyard and there was—my husband. Silently soaking up a few remaining hours of freedom before the start of another work week. Surrounded by a couple of tiki torches and a citronella candle. Scrunched up in a turtle-shaped kiddie pool he had pulled out of a dumpster. Man, you could not get more pathetic if you tried. Scooch over.

TECHNIQUE

Use image-editing software such as Adobe Photoshop or Paint Shop Pro to alter the color of the photos prior to getting prints. For journaling, mix computer fonts and hand-doodling. Print on white paper and color/distress with chalk and ink. Create title using WordArt in MS Word; flip direction so title appears in reverse and print on back of cardstock. (This ensures that the letters appear the right way on the front of the cardstock when cut out.) Cut out letters with scissors and a craft knife.

SUPPLIES

Patterned paper: Jeneva and Company; Cardstock: Bazzill; Kravitz computer font: scrapvillage.com; Chicken King computer font: fontdiner.com; Hattenschweiler computer font: Microsoft; Distress Ink: Ranger; Chalks: Craf-T Products; Letter stickers: Stickopotamus, Basic Grey; Colored markers: Sharpie; ClicknStick ACID-FREE Mounting Tabs: Therm O Web.

Leah Blanco Williams had always been into art, photos, and writing, so scrapbooking seemed like the next logical step. She didn't start truly enjoying the hobby, however, until she stopped taking to heart what she was told scrapbooking should be and instead decided what it would mean to her personally. The conclusion? "My pages are first and foremost for me," she says. "They are my own cathartic release and my own artistic expression. They are both deep and fluffy. They are right now." Blanco Williams was born and raised in Toronto, Canada. After graduating from York University, she moved to the United States to marry a cute boy named Thomas. She lives a simple life in Rochester, New York, with three dogs and a cockatiel named Chicken, and is currently obsessed with fixing up her house.

shoe
girl
lover

SHOE LOVER

MOTIVATION

To pay tribute to some of my favorite footwear. I smile just looking at them.
To document all the little things one might say about their shoes (i.e. respond with) if someone said, "Hey, nice shoes" (e.g. why I like them, where I got them, how much I got them for, etc.)

TIPS AND TECH

Prior to printing the journaling on the page, test on scrap paper to make sure the text is formatted as desired. Arrange photos over journaling and use clear fasteners to create flip-up. Attach ribbon with SuperTape and create title with letter stickers.

SUPPLIES

Ribbon: Carolee's Creations; Letter stickers: Memories Complete; Masked tape sticker: Pebbles Inc.; Flip Flop Fasteners: Destination Scrapbook Designs; SuperTape ACID-FREE Double-Sided Adhesive: Therm O Web.

DOES THIS DRESS... (CARD)

FROM PAGE 6
MOTIVATION

Seeing this die-cut in the store prompted me to turn to my bored-stiff husband and ask, "Hey, does this dress make her thighs look fat?" When it got a laugh out of him, I knew Glinda was coming home with me, and I had the makings of another handmade card.

TIPS AND TECH

Ink edges of patterned paper by dragging edge across ink pad, and arrange on card to make background.
Print journaling and cut into strips. Ink edges of strips. Chalk and heat emboss vellum to give Glinda's bubble color and shine. (Heat embossing involves pouring embossing powder over pigment ink and blasting it with a heat gun for a raised effect.)
Dab glitter glue on photo die cut, and allow at least 2 hours to dry. For inside of card, trim cardstock slightly smaller than surface and add punched shapes (a.k.a. "punchies").

SUPPLIES

Vellum: unknown; Patterned paper: Magenta, unknown; Cardstock: Bazzill; Cherry Coke computer font: scrapvillage.com; Glinda die cut: Paper House Productions; Versacolor Ink: Tsukineko; Star punches: unknown; Sticky Dots ACID-FREE Adhesive Sheets: Therm O Web; Chalk: Craf-T Products; Clear embossing powder: Anita's Embossing Powder; Stickles glitter: Ranger.

SILVER BALLET FLATS FROM LA REDOUTE.

STORAGE

TIME IS FLEETING

Here's a quick tech-talk on how acid, light, and air are your photos worst enemies and what you can do to help stop the "aging process"—Botox for your photos, if you will.

HAVING YOUR PHOTOS SURVIVE THE TEST OF TIME

Photographs are made up of several chemical layers—an emulsion, adhesive, and gelatin are the basics. Although these chemicals are relatively stable, they are vulnerable to certain environmental conditions. Sounds a lot like your old boyfriend!

OK, here are some tips to keep your precious print photos alive. Heat and humidity are not only notorious for dishing out some of the worst hair days in history, but they wreak havoc on your pics. If possible, photographs should not be kept in temperatures above 70 degrees Fahrenheit and relative humidity above 60%. Also avoid storage areas that have drastic changes in temperature—like what goes on in your attic or the trunk of your car. As far as the basement goes, if it's damp, it's not a good place for photo storage.

What we're trying to avoid here is fungus growth! Eeeek! A photograph's emulsion is made up of an organic material; hence heat and humidity make your photographs a virtual smorgasbord table, with that image of Aunt Mary's 75th birthday serving as a dessert tray.

So keep your photos stored in a cool, dry place. Of course, that may mean moving out of your five-floor walk-up, cold-water flat in the Lower East Side, but hey, your photos deserve the best, right?

What Is Acid and Acid-Free?

Acid is used in paper manufacturing to break apart the wood fibers and lignin, the substance that holds them together. If acid remains in the materials used for memory albums and pages, the acid can react chemically with photographs and accelerate their deterioration. Over time, acid breaks down the paper fibers, causing the paper to deteriorate and become brown and brittle. Paper from which the acid has been removed, so that it has a neutral 7.0 pH, is known as acid-free paper.

TWO MORE THINGS TO WORRY ABOUT

Air Pollutants

In-house air pollution can come from things like your household cleaners, cigarette smoke (yes, some people still indulge in a little tobacco), or your husband's underwear. So don't smoke in front of your photos, and keep them out of any closet harboring these pesky pollutants.

Ultraviolet Light

We hate to admit it, but it ain't good for our skin. And it ain't good for our pics, either. So as much your photographs may beg you to take them to the beach, be strict and just say "No!" And when they're home, keep them out of direct sunlight.

What Is Lignin and Lignin-Free?

Lignin is a naturally occurring substance found in plant life that helps provide strength within the plants by binding woody fibers together. Paper that contains large amounts of lignin (such as newsprint) is very acidic and will turn yellow when exposed to light and humidity. To be considered lignin-free, paper can contain a maximum of 1% lignin.

What Is Alkaline and Buffer?

Alkalinity is the opposite of acidity. Alkaline is the term used when something contains alkali or has a pH level of 7.0 or above. During the manufacturing process, an alkaline substance is added to the pulp, giving permanence and durability to the paper produced. Buffer is an alkaline substance—generally calcium carbonate (CaCO3)—added to the paper to make it acid-free.

What Is pH Factor?

The pH scale is the standard for measuring the acidity and alkalinity of a substance. The scale runs from 0 to 14, with each number representing a tenfold increase; 7.0 is considered neutral. Acid-free products have a pH factor of 7.0 or above. Special pens that test the pH level are available to help you determine the acidity or alkalinity of products.

What Is Archival Quality?

"Archival quality" is the term used to indicate materials that have undergone laboratory analysis to determine that their acidic and buffered content is within safe levels.

What Is Photo-Safe?

Similar to archival quality, the term photo-safe is more specific to materials used with photographs. Acid-free is the determining factor for a product to be labeled photo-safe.

WHITE-GLOVE TREATMENT

If at all possible, handle your photos with clean or gloved hands. Your hands are naturally acidic and register somewhere around 5.5 on the pH scale (black coffee comes in at 5). In other words, keep your grimy mitts off the pics.

LOCATION. LOCATION. LOCATION.

One word, baby. Acid. That's the killer. Get those photos out of shoeboxes. These are a virtual sarcophagus for your pics. The acid from the cardboard feasts on your pictures like worms dining on a corpse. Go out and get yourself archival-quality photo boxes and envelopes. These products are 100% acid-free and create an environment that will actually help stop any deteriorating processes that may have started.

If you're looking for something a little more high-tech, there are alternatives to hard copy. We're living in the digital age, and with it comes a variety of methods for storing your photos electronically. If you've got the time and energy (or the money, if you're willing to pay someone), you can embark on the laborious task of scanning all your images and storing them on CD-ROM or DVD. And a lovely bit of trivia to drop at your next cocktail party . . . sarcophagus literally means: "flesh-eating container."

People decide to scrapbook for a host of different reasons. Many times, this motivation determines the concepts they ultimately commit to paper—whether it's solely to pressing their family's history, to using it as therapy, to documenting a special time (good or bad), to just having fun, or everything in between.

I hope that the layouts at the beginning of the book have inspired you, helped you shed your inhibitions, quelled your apprehensions, and spanked your butt into action. It's time to let that internal scrapbook come out.

SOME INSPIRATION

If you still need a little more motivation, here are a few ideas to kick around.

The Misspent-Youth Scrapbook

Old concert-ticket stubs, malt-liquor labels, and a picture of the high school boy from the wrong side of the tracks you made out with.

The M.I.A. Scrapbook

Old friends and/or relatives who have dropped off the planet.

'The Cryptsters' Scrapbook

Documentation for your kids to prove that at one time you were cool.

The Plastic-Surgery Scrapbook

Sometimes looking good takes just a little help from modern medicine.

The "I Am a Goddess" Scrapbook

If a tree can grow in Brooklyn, surely a goddess can live in a downtown studio.

The Grace Kelly Look-Alike Scrapbook

C'mon, there have been times when, with the right scarf, sunglasses, and bobbed 'do you were her double. . .or at least were having just as much fun as the princess. The classiest scrapbook ever.

RAW FOOTAGE

GATHERING AND ORGANIZING YOUR PHOTOS AND OTHER VISUAL ELEMENTS

OK, so you've decided on your concept—now it's time to sift through years of "raw footage," gathering up the elements needed for your scrapbook. Begin collecting all items, no matter how obscurely related or ancillary to your topic. Photos, letters, matchbooks, ticket stubs, scraps of clothing, bills, hair, bullets, illustrations, news and magazines clippings, teeth, etc.

Sometimes there may be elements that you no longer have or may never have had. In that situation, I suggest you seek out those pieces by calling family members and/or old friends, shooting new photos, or logging on to ebay. Trust me, as much effort (I'm not talking endless hours) as you put into developing your scrapbook, the rewards reaped will be tenfold. Approach the project like the work of art it is, and give it the attention it deserves.

SHOULD IT STAY OR SHOULD IT GO

This is NOT the time to edit! At this stage of the game, when in doubt, DO NOT throw it out! In filmmaking, this concept is called coverage—it gives the editor and director options during the editing process, and it will give you the same creative options when putting together your scrapbook. This eclectic collecting style will also be one of the techniques you use in creating a truly unique finished product.

As you're gathering elements for the layout, the tone/concept/theme may appear to be going in a different direction than you had originally envisioned. Don't fight it. Go with it for a while—its final destination may result in a pleasant surprise. Like that time you ate Senegali food.

PREPRODUCTION

A FILMMAKER'S APPROACH TO CONSTRUCTING A SCRAPBOOK

There's an old saying in the film business: "The more of an amateur filmmaker you are, the more professionally you must run your production, and the best way to run a professional production is through preproduction."

Applying this concept to your scrapbooking will prove to be the difference between a scrapbook that merely displays your memories and one that inspires and captures the true essence of the moment you're bringing to scrap-life. In this chapter you will begin to use a filmmaker's sensibilities as you approach the early stages of creating your scrapbook. You will begin to assume the role of screenwriter/director in the process of unveiling your "story."

Theme

OK, you've decided the topic you want to scrap; now it's time to determine the all-important theme of your scrapbook. Always keeping your theme in play, will help keep your scrapbook focused and the sentiment you are trying to convey clear.

For example, let's say you've decided to scrap your first date with the guy who is now your husband. The theme might be "love conquers all" or "fate is a funny thing" or "opposites attract."

Think of a favorite movie, and boil it down to its most basic theme. Then realize how MOST of the scenes reinforce that theme; sometimes subtly, sometimes more obviously. Now think of your layout as a single scene in the feature-length movie you chose to scrap.

Every Picture Tells a Story

Like a great movie, every scrapbook should have a good storyline—one that is both entertaining and easily followed. The most basic elements a good storyline are a clear beginning, middle, and end. In film, these elements are the opening, the mid-point crisis, the turning point, and the climax.

Let's use the topic of Mary and Joe's First Date with "fate is a funny thing" as the theme. The beginning/opening is pretty clear: Establish the main characters and their situation. Mary and Joe as unlikely friends—fate—then as luvvahs. The mid-point crisis: Joe goes off to college. They break up—fate can be cruel. They no longer keep in touch.

Turning point: A few years later, Joe takes a job in NYC and meets Mary on the street—fate steps in again.

The Climax: They get married—you can't escape fate.

Edit! Edit! Edit!

Here we'll take a look at choosing the best images to convey your story and ways to use unconventional images and items that may be powerful emotional elements.

The mark of a good editor is a discerning eye—the ability to keep the story moving forward by using the most telling, interesting, and visually exciting images/elements available. While editing through your photos or elements, try to pick one that serves as the focal point of your layout, something that embodies the sentiment you are trying to convey. However, keep in mind that this element does NOT have to be the largest or positioned in the center of your layout.

Let's go back to Mary and Joe. Maybe there is a photo of Joe that is out of focus, or he is halfway out of the frame. This may be a great image to convey that Joe is leaving, or the disintegration of their relationship. Remember from Chapter 4, "When in doubt, DON'T throw it out." It's times like these when that adage will prove so true.

Also, suppose you have a diary entry of when Joe said he was leaving. That would be an excellent element to include during the mid-point-crisis section of your layout.

Indie Shorts to Epics

There are no rules on length (number of pages) or screen format (page size) that your scrapbook should run. However, there are some guidelines that can help you determine if it should be an "indie short" or an "epic five-reeler."

Some topics make the decision obvious. If you are documenting the last 100 years of your family history, you go long. If it's a one-night affair, maybe a single layout will suffice. Don't stretch a short concept, and don't shortchange an epic idea.

Storyboards

Even if your storyboards are nothing more than rough thumbnail sketches, you will find them extremely beneficial. First, they will help determine the number of pages you should devote to a given topic. Second, they will allow you literally to visualize each specific page in regard to photo, element, and type placement. Last, they will help you circumvent potential problems, all of which help you plan more exciting pages.

POETIC LICENSE

OK, so it really didn't happen that way, but man, it does make the scrapbook better. Do I rewrite history for the sake of entertainment? A resounding Yes! Well, maybe not resounding, 'cause it is contingent on the topic. However, if the topic is light or the facts are vague, always err on the side of sensationalism.

TOOLS OF THE TRADE

ESSENTIAL EQUIPMENT

I don't care how off-the-wall your scrapbooking style is—there are certain conventional tools that are essential to help create the layout you desire. This chapter is broken up into three sections that will give you a complete, albeit quick, look at some of the tools out there.

7 TOOLS EVERY SCRAPBOOKER SHOULD HAVE

1. Paper trimmer
2. Adhesive and adhesive remover
3. Scissors—conventional and decorative edge
4. Craft knife
5. Paper punch
6. Journaling pens
7. Scanner/printer (if available)

I NEED MORE

If you are one of those people who must have the latest and greatest—think Jimmy Choo's spring line of strappy sandals—there is a plethora of sites and stores out there with every conceivable scrapbooking item you could ever want. Check out Chapter 10 for a list of websites.

MY LUCKY SEVEN

We asked a variety of different scrapbookers, each with a distinctly different scrapbooking style and/or attitude, to give us seven "things" that they feel are essential to have close by when sitting down to scrap.

Dawn M. Mordarski

1. A set of medium-to-large alphabet stamps

A good set of alphabet stamps is not going to be cheap, but it's a great investment. Take the time to seek out a font that you really love, and you will use and reuse these stamps in a million different ways for years to come. I am a huge fan of Stampin' Up's lines of alphabet stamps, and I especially like the way they come unassembled, so you can put together the stamp based on how you're comfortable holding it.

2. The Internet

I'm not the most technologically-advanced girl, and I don't

scrap digitally yet. But the Internet has truly become an invaluable resource for me in my scrapping. I have used it to find inspiration—the layout galleries out there are impressive and widely varied (it's so cool to see what other folks are doing!), and there are technique articles, ideas, quotes, titles, how-to guides, organizational tips, and all other things scrap-related. Though I do love my small but slowly growing collection of books on scrapping, I have to say that you can learn almost anything you need to learn about scrapping over the Internet, thanks to wonderful, user-friendly sites.

3. Good-quality cardstock
This is an absolute must, especially in neutral colors, like black, cream, and a variety of whites and browns– with a few of your favorite brights. I love Stampin' Up's cardstock—it's dyed really well so the color is true throughout. I also love Bazzill Basics. And for more textured solids and the coolest patterns ever, I go to Basic Grey.

4. Sewing room stealings!
I grew up with a Grandma who was an amazing seamstress, and I love to use her sewing supplies in my scrapbooks—rickrack, ribbons, trimmings, and buttons are awesome for adding texture and dimension. Dress patterns make great background paper, especially for a page about a special dress, like a prom dress or a wedding gown.

5. Deckle-edged scissors
I have a huge rolling rack of different types of scissors with fancy edges. And yet, no matter how long I try to pick out some other cool pattern, I always, always, always end up using my deckle-edged scissors, which give the appearance of ripping but with evenness and flow that I love. They are a great neutral look—I can make their design say anything!

6. A good working scrap bin
My scrap bin has become the center of my scrapping life. I do not throw any paper out, ever, unless is it truly ruined in some way. I figure if I am going to do paper crafts, then it is my responsibility as a person to make sure I do not waste paper. That was the intention behind having a scrap bin. But the outcome has been that I've learned how a tiny bit of patterned paper can make a huge punch. I've learned how to print onto scrap paper from my computer, and I've found that my scrapbooks have benefited from the repetition of certain pieces of paper—as I keep and use scraps, they provide repetition and rhythm that help move along the stories in my books.

7. Creativity
You don't have to be a crafty person to scrapbook. You don't have to have good handwriting, or lots of supplies, or an artsy eye. You have to have creativity.

SCRAPBOOK-ING A TO ZSIAGE™

Don't feel bad— you're not the only kid on the block who doesn't know your craft knife from your vellum. Here's a quick rundown of some key terms.

What Are Sheet Protectors?

Sheet protectors are made of polypropylene and slip over a finished album page. They can be side-loading or top-loading and fit all sizes, including the most popular 8" x 11" or 12" x 12" pages. It is important that they be acid-free and PVC-free. Use those specifically labeled photo-safe or archival quality.

What Are Paper Trimmers?

Excellent for quick, straight cutting, trimmers are extremely handy and save loads of time, but you need to choose a good one! It is especially important to choose a brand that cuts straight—and you'll be surprised that some of them don't! Look for these features: an extension arm that will accommodate 12" x 12" pages; replaceable blades; a grid system making cutting and measuring easy. Tricky but not necessarily vital extras include blades that score, perforate, or cut fancy edges. Cutterpede and Zision are excellent paper trimmers; however, it is a personal preference, so try a few before you decide what to purchase.

What Is a Craft Knife?

This utility knife is used free-hand and perfect for cutting precisely a variety of shapes. Craft knives create a crisp cut and prevent small snags and tears on your paper projects. Change the blade frequently for constant precise cutting.

What Are Decorative-Edge Scissors?

There is a huge variety of scissors with decorative edges that you can use on paper to create a design. These are a personal preference.

What Are Paper Punches?

Punches are available to accommodate virtually every design imaginable. Punches actually "punch" the design through paper to create a die-cut. Once again, a personal preference.

What Are Die-Cut Systems?

These hand-held or desktop machines cut a variety of letters and shapes out of paper, or any material that is "die-cut-able." SIZZIX and QUICKUTZ are two brands that are very popular.

What Are Templates?

Templates are patterns or stencils, usually made of plastic or that have a cut pattern, used as a guide in making something accurately.

What Is Cardstock?

This is the backbone of your scrapbook pages. Heavier than standard paper, cardstock is excellent for creating every type of scrapbook page. Many, many, many colors are available.

Zsiage™, LLC was founded in 2005 and is headquartered in Bayside, New York. They are a manufacturer and supplier of high quality paper crafting products, and they plan to deliver outstanding service to the independent retailer worldwide. Product lines include thirteen awareness papers, twelve Asian-inspired papers, eight Italian-inspired papers, eight eclectic papers, and six martini papers. For more information about the company or products, call (718) 224-1976 or visit www.zsiage.com.

What Is Patterned Paper?

Patterned paper is pre-printed paper, usually sporting a repeated design. You'll discover that the patterns can range from subtle white-on-white designs to day-glo juvenile images and everything in between.

MOUNTING AND ADHESIVE SYSTEMS

The humble glue stick is inexpensive and versatile when you're just starting out. As you get into scrapping, you will find that several different adhesives will be useful in your kit. From repositionable adhesives to permanent glues that provide a strong bond for plastic or metal, there is an adhesive on the market for every job you'll ever conceive of. Here are just a few:

Double-sided or Mounting Tape

This comes on a roll or in a traditional tape dispenser, in tabs or slivers dispensed from a box or plastic container, or that perhaps the most convenient of all, the tape runner. Look for dispensers that are refillable. Double-sided tape is absolutely invaluable for all sorts of adhesion. Four tabs are sufficient to adhere a photo, or a line of tape will effectively stick down the entire edge. Brands to look for: Herma, Xyron, Pritt.

Dimensional Glue

This allows you to create a dimensional aspect to your work by raising the elements above the page.

The glue is also great for adhering buttons and metal embellishments. Brand: Helmar Liquid Scrap Dots.

Foam Tape

A double-sided tape with foam layers for three-dimensional effects. Available in sheets, rolls, pre-cut dots, or squares.

Vellum Spray

This is a spray adhesive that can be used to invisibly adhere materials like vellum and acetate. It is an acid-free formula which is repositionable and odorless. Brand: Helmar V2 Vellum Adhesive.

Clear Drying Glue

This is useful for invisibly adhering transparent elements like resin or glass bubbles. Be careful when applying: Even though it dries clear, it can be seen if you make little splotches. Brands: KI Memories Gloo; Plaid Dimensional Magic; Helmar Gemstone Glue.

Repositionable Adhesive

If you like a second chance at getting things right, the Herma Dotto Removable Glue Dispenser is something you shouldn't live without. It provides a strong but temporary hold and can even be removed by rubbing with your fingers. No mess! Scotch makes a restickable adhesive glue stick, and the fabulous Sailor 2 in 1 Glue allows you to choose if you want a permanent or temporary hold, depending on how long you leave it to dry.

Zip Dry Paper Glue

This defies belief. It is a liquid glue that does not wrinkle paper, ever! It is just magic on paper and photos and can also be used for glitter, beads, wire and metal stampings.

HIRING THE CREW

TECHNICAL NEEDS OF YOUR SCRAPBOOK

In the previous chapter, we took a brief tour through some of the conventional products that can make your life easier, help achieve the look you're after, and even shed light on a hidden star-element of your layout.

Let's take a quick look at a few tips and techniques using these tools that will help you achieve the scrapbook you envision.

Stencils and Rub-on Lettering

So you hate your handwriting. No problem—let stencils do the work for you.

Cropping

Try as you might, you will not always create the perfect composition in your camera lens. When arranging photographs on your layout, creative decisions will need to be made. To crop or not to crop, that is the question. A word of warning, though: You should NEVER crop an original photograph for which you have no negative. Duplicate it, and then feel free to crop to your heart's content.

A pair of L-shaped croppers are ideal for this task. Make them yourself from heavyweight black cardstock. When placed over a photograph, the croppers can be moved around to view how and where you can cut the pic. You'll see where the focus of the image is and how it will appear before you make any cuts.

Framing

Once your photographs have been reduced or enlarged, you can frame them. The most common technique: Create a mat by adhering the photograph to a larger piece of paper or cardstock, leaving a border around. When using patterned papers, it helps distinguish the photo from the background. Lightning-quick tip: Adhere your photograph to one corner of a piece of cardstock, then simply cut the remaining two sides.

There are many other ways to frame photos and sometimes it is enough to use simple photo corners. The clear ones "invisibly" adhere your photograph, with the added bonus that it can be removed and no adhesive touches the photo (especially important for heritage photographs).

You can use vellum to frame a not-so-great photograph that, for sentimental reasons, you don't want to cut up. Cut vellum to the same size as the photo then cut a shape in the vellum to reveal the best part of your picture.

Sewing

Machine-stitching on pages looks hip. Use stitching as a purely cosmetic device or as a practical way to join layers of paper together. Use straight stitch and zig-zag stitches—and for best results, a denim needle is recommended. If you don't have one on hand, just use a nice, sharp needle. To prevent your stitching from undoing, leave long threads at the beginning and end and secure at the back of your work with tape.

Hand-stitching gives a terrific hand-made look. It also allows you to use fibers and thicker yarns that won't go through your sewing machine. Tricky technique: Run your paper through a sewing machine without any thread in it to create evenly-spaced holes through which you can hand-stitch.

EMBELLISHING

Decorative Cutting

Use decorative edgers (scissors) to create a little interest on your pages. By offsetting the blade, you can create different decorative effects. Use pinking edgers to create a ric-rack look using textured cardstock.

Punches and Die Cuts

Using paper punches or a die-cut system allows you to create shapes quickly and in multiples. This would otherwise take hours with scissors or a craft knife, and you would tear your hair out. Circle and square punches are incredibly versatile and useful to keep in your kit, to mat small photos and to create repetitive design elements on pages. Your local craft store will most likely have a die-cut system in its workshop for customers to use. The shapes available are endless and suitable for all sorts of occasions.

AGING

WARNING: If you don't like the idea of setting to your newly completed layouts with sandpaper, stain, or a match, turn the page promptly.

Sanding

This is a simple way to make your artwork look like it has seen a few family viewings. Use regular sandpaper from the hardware store, or buy a purpose-made sanding block at scrapbook suppliers. Go easy at first—it doesn't take much to sand a big hole in your hard work. Buff off the edges, and select other parts of the pages that might naturally get a little wear and tear. Sanding can be used very

effectively with techniques like dog-earing and inking. Perhaps you should just leave your work in the hands of the nearest kids over mealtime and to get the age-old effect pronto!

Inking

Scrunch you paper up, uncrumple it, then apply ink, paint, tea, or coffee to age the paper. A spritz of water allows the color to run in a strangely satisfying way. Throw caution to the wind; the messier the better. Dry with a hot-air gun or iron to prevent warping.

Flame Grill!

Smoky effects and burnt edges can be authentically achieved, but take care! Remove as much residual soot as possible, and spray with a fixative agent. This is not recommended for originals. If you are not into danger, get the same results by inking a torn edge or Photoshopping digital images.

WRITE THE WORDS

This is sometimes the most difficult part. What to say? Start with facts: dates, name, places. Remember, all those martinis can affect your memory, so this way you will never forget your mother-in-law's name. Seriously though, for future generations it will be important to identify the people in your photos when you are gone. So, you hate your handwriting, let's not go there just yet. Here are some other possibilities:

Use the Computer

Loads of fonts are available. Wild and crazy typefaces can be found to suit any style of page. To print journal boxes and labels for your pages, use scraps of cardstock. Compose your words, choose font and point size, and print onto scrap paper. Approved? Then use a repositionable adhesive to stick a piece of cardstock directly over the printed words on your draft copy and whizz it through the printer again. Voilá!

Top Tips

For acetate or vellum, use the "draft quality" option on your computer. The ink tends to sit on the surface of these papers rather than being immediately absorbed, so to save the temptation of touching before the ink is dry, print as the last thing at night and leave to dry, untill the morning.

For eye-catching headings, stencils, alphabet stamps, and rub-on letters are perfect. Alphabet stamps are available either mounted or unmounted.

For something random, mix more than one style of font. Rub-on letters are super-easy to use. As with the other styles of headings, it's useful to mark out with pencil just to avoid running off the page. Stencils are versatile because they can be chalked, embossed, stippled, or outlined to give different looks. They are inexpensive too. And now to hand-writing at some point you should include your own handwriting in a scrapbook for posterity. A prize-winning or family-favorite recipe might be an easy way to start. If committing your thoughts and feelings to paper seems intimidating and too revealing, a cunning use of secret journal boxes is the answer. Hidden behind photos, pockets, or embellishments, they are not visible for the whole world to read.

Paper and Backgrounds

Many scrapbookers believe that the paper/cardstock is one of the most essential elements and the "anchor" of your layout. I have to say that I agree with this sentiment only partially, and I'll tell you why. Scrappers have come to rely too heavily on existing themed paper stocks to convey their message and fail to use more obscure and inventive backgrounds in their layouts. So, my one suggestion to you is to check out what the stores have to offer but also let your imagination run wild. Try digging up original and novel backgrounds to anchor your layouts and the sentiment you are trying to get across.

What? You need an example? OK, how about this. Let's say you're doing a layout on ex-boyfriends, and you want it to be relatively light and amusing. However, in retrospect, you realize these guys were cads, to say the least. How about using something unusual as a back-ground—like the court papers filed by the State of California in the Ted Bundy trial? It's easy enough to find on ebay, and I'm sure you won't find that at your local scrapbooking store.

All I'm saying is to keep an open mind and a sharp eye when deciding on potential back-grounds for your layouts.

CROP AND PRINT

COMMIT YOUR IMAGES AND ELEMENTS TO PAPER

OK, we've given you a brief background on what a scrapbook is, and shown you some tricks and tools of the trade; and hopefully, the layouts you've seen in this book have inspired you to go out and create some of your own. Now it's time to loosen the apron strings. Not totally cut them yet, but loosen them.

As you can see by the layouts we've presented, no single style or set of rules need be followed when creating your scrapbook page. You must find your own "style artistique." However, you must also remember that scrapbooking is a visual art form, and your decision on how to lay out the elements should be determined by two things: The best way to tell your story and the most visually captivating.

Here are a few final considerations to keep in mind when approaching your page.

Fade Up

Think of your first page as the opening scene. This page is crucial in continuing to convey the tone established by your cover and/or to establish the tone to be conveyed throughout the rest of the book.

Framing

Imagine your layout page as a frame of film, as if you were looking through the viewfinder of a camera. Try to visualize the page with a foreground and background. Consider images entering the page from the sides, and always consider the use of "white space" (leaving parts of the page free of images or type).

Voice-Over

Besides photos, artwork, and memorabilia, there are a host of elements available to help tell your story. However, the words you choose, the fonts you pick, and their positioning on the page can either add to your story or become a distraction (and/or render it hokey).

Pacing

If you are creating a multi-page scrapbook, keep in mind these certain concepts. Are you building to a climax? Is there some kind of humorous payoff? Are you creating a "slow-motion" mood of emotion? Experiment with ways to excite your readers/viewers into racing through pages en route to the big bang or lulling them into a state of reflection. Great places of inspiration are fine art and art-photography books. Study how painters and photographers render and capture elements on the canvas and in the frame to create an instant emotional reaction.

Establishing Shot

You've pasted down your final photo . . . the scrapbook is complete! It tells the story of your pain, your joy, your good times or bad. It is from the heart, and you should be proud of it. But it needs an original cover. That's the world's first impression of your work.

Your scrapbook cover acts like the opening shot of a film. The medium you use to create the cover, the images you place upon it, the titling, size, and binding or just the simple color(s) you choose are all essential in setting an initial tone—funny, romantic, dramatic, bittersweet, etc. It's time to step back and review the scrapbook. Maybe you had an initial cover in mind, and now you feel it's not right? Maybe you feel it needs a simple black cover? Just don't shortchange the effort you put into creating your cover. It doesn't need to be elaborate, but it should be reflective of the sentiment nestled on the pages.

171

THE AMERICAN SCRAPBOOK CENTER*

In less time than it takes to get your roots done (and for a lot less money), you can create a scrapbook that when seen by friends, family, and colleagues, will surely make them green with envy, give you the edge with your sibling rivalry, and guarantee a raise at work.

Well, maybe the guaranteed raise is a bit of a stretch, but you never know!

Before you start, we are going to assume that you've organized your photos and negatives. We've already talked about labeling and storing your photos and negatives in archival-safe photo-storage boxes or a "safe" binder with "safe" sheet protectors. And we've discussed ways to organize your photos chronologically by theme or event and use dividers to label them.

What!? You haven't done that? Well, don't sweat it; you can still start scrapbooking.

PLAN YOUR THEME AND LAYOUT

Decide what you want to scrap. What type of theme do you want to create? Friends? Vacation? Dating disasters? Baby? Divorce? Special event? Think of it as if you are narrating a story. Do you want a single- or double-page layout, or both? How many photos do you want to use? One or several? Make sure you choose one photo that is your focal point. It doesn't have to be the biggest, just strategically placed so that the other photos (if any) will flow on the page or pages.

LET'S DO IT

1. Select the photos you would like to use, and choose a theme for the layout you would like to create. Usually two to four photos fit on one page and four to six photos fit on a two-page spread. Remember, you do not have to scrap every picture you have—select only your favorite photos to highlight the event, feeling, or moment you want to convey.

2. Select acid-free paper that will complement colors found in the photographs. Experiment with different color combinations of cardstock and/or patterned paper to find the perfect colors that will enhance your photographs.

*AMERICAN SCRAPBOOKING CENTER of Bayside, New York, is owned by Dina Quondamatteo-Berardi and has quickly become one of the main centers for scrapbooking in the New York metropolitan area. Visit www.americanscrapbookingcenter.com for more info.

30-MINUTE SCRAPBOOK

3. Choose one photo to be your focus. As a general rule, try to select sharp-image photos with bright colors and well-lit subjects.

4. Shape and mat your photos to add extra prominence to your focal point. You can do this by matting your photo with a wider border than the others. You can also double- or triple-mat the photo. Decide on the shape of your photo. While shaping your photos, keep in mind that simple shapes such as squares, rectangles, circles, or ovals are most eye-pleasing.

Use an acid-free and photo-safe adhesive to place the photo onto a piece of paper that is slightly larger. If you want to double- and triple-mat your photo, follow the same rule of thumb, making the next mat larger than the last to create the effect. You can vary the widths of the mats to add more or less prominence to the photo.

Another mat style is cutting your paper with decorative-edged scissors. If irrelevant details appear in the background, simply trim them out. Remember, this doesn't mean you have to cut out all of the background. Some ordinary items pictured in the background will bring a flood of memories essential to journaling and reminiscing, so don't trim unnecessarily.

5. Add journaling—a MUST and VERY IMPORTANT! No page is complete without adding your thoughts, feelings, and experiences. Take a few minutes to write down not only the "who" and "when" but also the "how," "what," and "why." Write what you remember and how you felt/feel about the photos/event!

6. Arrange photos, journaling, and titles on your page before you affix them. Well-designed pages are balanced and will follow a flow that mimics a backward "S." Make certain that you are pleased with the layout. Then simply secure the elements onto the page.

Congratulations! You've successfully completed your first scrapbook pages! Now go out and break every rule we've just taught you.

100+ SITES

EVERYTHING FROM THE CHEAPEST PRICE ON CRAFT SCISSORS TO GRABBING
SOME GRAPHIC INSPIRATION.

www.1001freefonts.com

www.acmoore.com

www.advantus.com

www.amandablu.com

www.americanscrapbookingcenter.com

www.apple.com/itunes.com

www.archivalmethods.com

www.arcticfrog.net

www.arnoldgrunmmer.com

www.artgirlz.com

www.autumnleaves.com

www.basicgrey.com

www.bazzillbasics.com

www.bizrate.com

www.bombshells.com

www.chatterboxinc.com

www.cloud9design.biz

www.coopstuff.com

www.craftsetc.com

www.createforless.com

www.creativexpress.com

www.cropaholics.com

www.dafont.com

www.dateitpaper.com

www.deluxecuts.com

www.designbutcher.com

www.deviantart.com

www.digitalphotos101.com

www.digitalscrapbookdesigns.com

www.digitalscrapbookpreviews.com

www.diynetwork.com

www.enchantedmercantile.com

www.editorskeys.com

www.epson.com

www.flaxart.com

www.fontwerks.com

www.gauchogirl.com

www.genealogicaljourneys.com

www.goweststudios.com

www.graffiti.org

www.graphicus.co.uk

www.havanastreet.com

www.heidigrace.com

www.hgtv.com

www.hipchixstudios.com

www.houseind.com

www.hp.com

www.invokearts.com

www.istockphoto.com

www.joann.com

www.judikins.com

www.karenfosterdesign.com

www.kodomoinc.com

www.lildavisdesigns.com

www.littlebit.com

www.looseends.com

www.lucky13apparel.com

www.MacScrapbook.com

www.magicscraps.com

www.mara-mi.com

www.marthastewart.com

www.mayaroad.com

www.michaels.com

www.moma.org

www.musee-online.org

www.myenchantedscrapbook.com

www.nrndesigns.com

www.offray.com

www.paperaddict.com

www.papersalon.com

www.pattiewack.com

www.pearlpaint.com

www.pebblesinc.com

www.plaidonline.com

www.popcultmag.com

www.printfile.com

www.provocraft.com

www.queenandcompany.com

www.quickutz.com

www.redvelvetart.com

www.retroadart.com

www.sassafraslass.com

www.save-on-crafts.com

www.scrapalatte.net

www.scrapbook.com

www.scrapbook-bytes.com

www.scrapbookdiva.com

www.scrapbookdreamer.com

www.scrapbooking-directory.com

www.scrapbookingguide.com

www.scrapbookingsuppliesonline.com

www.scrapbooks.com

www.scrapbooksally.com

www.scrapbooksuperstore.com

www.scrapgirls.com

www.scrapjazz.com

www.scraptown.com

www.scrapvillage.com

www.scrapworks.com

www.sevengypsies.com

www.simplescrapbooksmag.com

www.stampingontheritz.com

www.stewartgill.com

www.tattoo-art.com

www.tensecondsstudio.com

www.tradecards.com

www.twopeasinabucket.com

www.utrechtart.com

www.zbeckybrown.com

www.zsiage.com